FLY HIGH, RUN FREE

By the Same Author

*

THROUGH THE BADGER GATE

Fly High, Run Free

JANE RATCLIFFE

With a Foreword by
VIRGINIA McKENNA

1979
CHATTO & WINDUS
LONDON

Published by
Chatto & Windus Ltd
40 William IV Street
London WC2

*

Clarke, Irwin & Co. Ltd
Toronto

*British Library Cataloguing
in Publication Data*

Ratcliffe, Jane
  Fly high, run free
  1. Wildlife rescue – England – Lake District
  1. Title
  636.08'3   OL83.2
  ISBN 0–7011–2365–6

Printed in Great Britain by
Ebenezer Baylis and Son Ltd.,
The Trinity Press, Worcester, and London

*This book is dedicated to
all those wild creatures who came my way
and gave me their confidence and trust
while I cared for them,
and who are now living and breeding
in the Cumbrian countryside*

Contents

Illustrations

Foreword

A few weeks ago I asked a naturalist friend of mine if he knew of a Mrs. Ratcliffe who lived in Cheshire and was concerned with the rehabilitation of injured wild creatures to their natural environment. 'Indeed I do,' he replied. 'She is really good news.'

Everyone reading this account of Mrs. Ratcliffe's work with wildlife must surely endorse this opinion. The lack of sentimentality in her approach to her patients is an indisputable sign of her real love for them, and of her deep concern that, whenever possible, the injured animal or bird should be returned to its own habitat.

As one reads the stories in this simply and directly written book, it is all too clear that real love and concern are vital to this kind of work. A quick emotional response to an animal in need can often as quickly fade when one is faced with the prospect of weeks and often months of broken nights, nursing, feeding and teaching. But whether in her handling of newborn hedgehogs, her instruction of tawny owls in the capture of live prey, or in her personally rewarding experience in the rehabilitation of kestrels, Mrs. Ratcliffe proves over and over again that any creature that finds itself in her hands is more than fortunate.

Perhaps the thing which strikes one most about this book is the author's lack of self— an unusual characteristic of first person, real-life sagas. All her energies, mental and physical, are directed towards the animals and their well-being. She is a woman of action.

In the world we live in today where the majority of people think of little else but themselves, it is both refreshing and uplifting to enter for a while Mrs. Ratcliffe's world where, thanks to her, most of the creatures she has cared for have been able once again to Fly High, Run Free.

Virginia McKenna

Preface

As man's influence extends across our diminishing wild places
the pressures on Nature are ever increasing. All of us have a
duty to protect our wildlife and help it to survive.

Saving injured creatures and restoring them to the wild has
been a lifelong concern of mine. In this book I have tried not
only to show what can be achieved but also to emphasize the
specialized knowledge and patient work involved in caring for
and releasing mammals and birds for a successful new life
amongst their own kind.

I do not want to encourage everyone who finds a displaced
nestling to take it home. On the contrary, wild creatures should
be left to their parents' care, and only when injured or proved
to be deserted may they be taken into the care of an experienced
person. The advice of a veterinary surgeon should then be sought
and, if the case is not straightforward, it should be passed on
to somebody with the knowledge and time to give the necessary
care and the proper training.

A wild creature should never be taken into captivity. Thanks
to the work of dedicated conservationists, such an act is now
often illegal.

I have not mentioned the cost of my work, but one should
not overlook the expense of feeding stuffs, professional medical
advice and treatment, the construction of suitable, roomy
aviaries and so on.

Finally, I must say, by way of encouragement, that to see a
once-crippled bird flying high, or mammal running free, is one
of the greatest joys that life can give.

Acknowledgements

I am indebted to all the friends who have helped me, both with their encouragement and their interest in my activities, and in particular to Brian Coles, B.V.Sc., for his patient and skilful work and for the use of his X-ray films; to Marion Browne for her enthusiasm and help with badgers; to John Webster, Co-Badger Recorder for Cumbria, for his interest and help with release of birds and information on barn owls; to Tony Warburton for showing me his work with barn owls, for his help with a difficult sparrow hawk and for letting me use some of his unpublished work; to Stuart Wilkinson for his endless patience in rehabilitating several very difficult humanized kestrels back to the wild; to Simon of Summerhill for the use of his barns for housing, and his help in feeding and releasing several barn owls and other birds of prey; to Jean Bryne for care and interest in nursing one of my kestrels at her home; to Tony Crittenden, my local R.S.P.C.A. Inspector, for his help, concern and devotion to wildlife; to Terry Wells for temporarily taking over my pair of breeding barn owls; to Colin Armitstead, Ray Eades, Paul Williams and David Woodward, for ringing my birds before release; and to all the farming friends who have given up their barns for a season while establishing pairs of my aviary-bred barn owls and their young into the wild.

I am also indebted to Mary and Joe Eastwood and Dorothy Barton in whose woodland much of my work has been done.

I am grateful also to the Editors of *Wildlife Magazine* and the *Hawk Trust Report* for permission to include my material first published by them; to the British Field Sports Society; to Roger Burrows, Tony Soper and John Sparks for permitting me to use references from their works; to Sylvia Trevor for allowing me to use the work of the late Frances Pitt; also to Brian

ACKNOWLEDGEMENTS

Vesey-Fitzgerald for helpful suggestions and permission to quote from his work, and to Michael Houston for his stimulating articles and his permission to quote from one of them.

Lastly, and by no means least, I acknowledge with gratitude and appreciation the help I have received from my husband in my work with wildlife, and for constructing the aviaries and badger compound, editing my manuscript and taking the photographs to illustrate this book.

E.J.R.

I

Freedom and Flight

From an early age I have always had the urge to be out in the open. As I watched the birds enjoying the limitless space above me, and the animals living in the freedom of the countryside, I became convinced that all wild creatures belonged in the open and that none should be held in captivity.

Whenever injured birds and mammals are put in my care now it is always my aim to restore them to health without taming them in any way, so that they can return to their natural environment. My great reward has always been to see the bird flying high, or the animal running free, as it returned to its own life and forgot the human being who had saved it.

After a lifetime of working with animals I am now sure that my method of caring without taming, and feeding on the natural food of the type found in the wild, has achieved great success in the curing and rehabilitating of injured birds and mammals.

At the age of ten I nursed the humble sparrows which flitted in and out of our grimy town garden and the house mouse which came out of the hole in the kitchen floor beside the old range. I soon discovered that much could be done to help injured wild creatures, although at that age good intentions were sometimes more in evidence than skill.

The observation of wildlife in its own surroundings has always interested me, and as a small child I used to go to the local pond with my fishing net. One fine spring morning, the air fresh despite the industrial atmosphere of our Yorkshire town, my mother, busy during the school holidays, sent me out to play. With a small goldfish bowl on a string and a fishing net in my hand, I went down the rough track behind the house, past the river, polluted by the effluent from the nearby blanket mills, and along a path through a strip of tussocky grass to the pond. The first spikes of rosebay willow herb were pushing through the vegetation, and later in the season bright pink flowers would add colour to prove that life existed in this grimy landscape. Rhubarb was a much grown crop in the area and my miniature wildlife reserve—my pond—lay in one of the rhubarb fields. From previous visits I knew that it contained small grey fish.

I found a safe place on the bank from which to lower my net, and filled my bowl with pond water and bits of weed. Hopefully, and rather dreamily, I passed my net to and fro in the dark water. I did not expect to catch anything so soon on my first outing, but to my amazement when I pulled the net from the water I found I had caught a small grey fish with sharp spines running down its back—a stickleback. Imagine my surprise when, on opening the net fully, I discovered a second fish with a fiery red breast. It was quite the most beautiful creature I had ever seen and even more wonderful considering the ugly surroundings. I popped the two fish into my bowl and continued my search. Eventually I caught another red-breast stickleback and added this bright little fish to the others in the bowl.

I now realize that this fiery stickleback must have awakened my interest in the animal world. This was the first living creature I can remember studying.

Triumphantly I went home and showed the fish to my mother. I had already decided where I was going to put them, and they were certainly not going to stay in their small bowl. Too many tiddlers end their days in such containers. My father had given me a large glass accumulator tank and much against my mother's wishes this was set up with gravel, stones and plenty of weed to form a natural habitat for my fish. Hours of watching their movements showed that the two red-breasted sticklebacks were males and in breeding condition. This made my aquarium all the more exciting. I read about these fishes and was overjoyed to find that in my hunt I had caught such interesting specimens. The stickleback is one of the most fascinating of pond breeds and their subsequent behaviour proved no disappointment.

As they settled down to their life in the aquarium, the two red-breasts showed distinct signs of claiming their territory. Each took possession of one end of the tank, marking an invisible boundary line down the centre over which either passed at his peril.

Outside the breeding season, sticklebacks are not really aggressive. They may vie for food, but otherwise live a quiet life in small shoals. Once the breeding season comes round, they defend their territory vigorously. The males acquire their brilliant nuptial breasts, and this colouring arouses hostility in another male if it trespasses on his territory. The defender usually delivers only a threat as he darts towards the trespasser, his mouth wide open as if to bite and with the three dorsal spines erect, like a dog raising its hackles. If this is an insufficient threat, the defending fish performs a different movement that can culminate in a fight on the territorial boundary. Head downwards, hovering in a jerky manner, spines erect, he positions himself as though he were about to scoop along the sand on the bottom of the tank. If a fight follows and the defender holds his territory, the loser goes off to make his nest elsewhere.

To make his nest the little red-breast on the left of my tank proceeded to move mouthfuls of sand from the rear corner to form a small pit. On this he made a neat round egg-shaped nest with a horizontal hole through the centre by collecting fine pieces of water weed and glueing them together with a sticky secretion produced by the kidneys. Once the nest was complete the male assumed an even brighter colouring. The red became more intense and his back became a shiny bluish hue, making him extremely conspicuous. Meanwhile, the little grey female was swollen with eggs and the male, in his fine nuptial dress, swam in a leaping display around her, enticing her into his ball-shaped nest in a performance similar to that of, for example, bower birds. It seemed incredible that such a lowly form of pond life could also behave in such an attractive and elaborate manner.

Now that she was ready, the female accepted his offer and followed him, pushing her way into the nest so that only her head and tail protruded. The male hovered around behind her, occasionally nudging her tail as if to give encouragement, while she laid her eggs. The female then left the nest and the male immediately entered to fertilize her eggs. From then on the little grey female took no further part in the upbringing of her young. The male guarded the nest and, swimming as though suspended within, would remain there fanning a current of fresh water over the eggs with alternate strokes of his pectoral fins, to ensure that they were properly aerated. If the other red-breast stickleback came too near to the family territory, the male would dart out and drive him off, returning to fan the eggs and carry on the parental duties.

I became engrossed in my observations, and the holiday came to an end all too soon. Suddenly I realized that my absorbing study must stop. My mother could not bother with such things during the term time, so reluctantly I trekked back to the pond and carefully launched my fish into the wild. As I returned to my country boarding school I wondered about the fate of my family of sticklebacks.

At Casterton School in Westmorland—now Cumbria—my mind often wandered far away from my schoolroom desk. I used to dream of the short time each week I could go out wandering in the country. We were never allowed out alone, so I had a standing arrangement with three like-minded school-friends that instead of games we should spend each Saturday afternoon in quiet walks scanning the hedgerows and fields for interesting wildlife.

On one occasion we noticed a row of swallows perched on the boundary fence of a field. Eight of these dark blue birds sat and preened on the top rail, twittering together in swallow fashion, and occasionally flitting round the field. To see how close we could get before they took wing and landed elsewhere, we stalked across a field of buttercups, cow parsley and milkmaids, creeping nearer and nearer to the birds. The last fifteen yards made all the difference as first one bird and then the next took to the air. My friends soon lost their birds. At last only one of the two that I was allotted to try and touch was still perched on the fence. I moved up to a few feet from my swallow, stopping to watch it closely. Still it did not fly away. Its brilliant metallic blue plumage was iridescent in the sunshine, and above its white breast was a deep red throat patch and forehead with a blue bib to match its back.

Slowly, not once taking my eyes from the bird, I stretched my hand towards it, moving closer all the time, until I stood right in front. Passing my hand behind, I touched its back. As it never lifted its wings, I closed my fingers gently round it and took it to my friends who were anxious to know what was happening. When I opened my hand it lay as though dead on my outstretched palm, and we examined it closely, suspecting sickness. But how could it be sick for we had just seen it flying around with the others? Then, with a twitter, it stretched out its wings and flew off to join its mates. As it spread its tail wide, the swallow revealed the graceful, long outer tail streamers, forming between them a smooth curve of white dots on the metallic blue plumage. On our return no one believed we had picked a fast-flying swallow off a fence, examined it and let it free. Perhaps my slow staring approach mesmerized it.

The next spring I was determined to find a swallow's nest, and my observations led me to an outbuilding in a nearby farm, where a swallow was repeatedly flying through a broken window. I stood quietly inside in a dark corner and saw the bird return time after time to plaster small pieces of mud onto a ledge just under the roof, until a nest was formed. I watched many times as the eggs were laid and hatched and the three youngsters developed. Towards the end there was great excitement as the young took turns out on the beam, flapping their wings furiously, while their parents arrived every five minutes with fresh food caught on the wing. The next evening when I looked in, the nest was empty and all five birds could be seen skimming over the treetops, flitting about in the sky, the parents frequently passing food to the young. All the fledglings had an immediate mastery of flight, and, since their outer streamers had not yet developed, their only recognizable feature, apart from the parents feeding them, was their short tail feathers.

These experiences with swallows aroused my interest in birds and I began to take more and more notice of them, studying seriously the reasons for their behaviour and evolution.

One bird seldom seen at close quarters is the swift, a rather weird creature with long scythe-shaped wings and very rapid and tireless flight, that seldom lands except at the nest. According to David Lack, in his book *Swifts in a Tower*, they sometimes sleep on the wing, rising on a thermal several hundred feet up, eventually returning to the insect level where they feed. If they do not breed in the first year, they are thought to remain on the wing for many months until they finally come to rest under the eaves of buildings, in holes or on rocky ledges, to build their nests. Their nesting material like their insect food is also collected on the wing.

At school on warm summer evenings I used to watch fascinated and enthralled as the swifts streaked across the sky with flickering wing beats, screaming and shrieking round the buildings in their large family parties. My first close encounter with this species came from a nest under the eaves of my home one summer holiday.

For three years this nest site at the side of our house had been used by a family of swifts, despite competition from sparrows. In fact each year I used to place two cardboard shoe boxes, minus their ends, side by side just inside the loft under the eaves so that the sparrows could take their pick and still leave room for the swifts.

Returning home from church one wet Sunday morning the sad sight of a very wet and bedraggled swift floundering in a puddle met our eyes. Without pausing to change out of my best clothes, I gathered the wet bundle in my hands and wrapped it in a tea towel from the kitchen—the first dry cloth I could find—hoping my mother would not want to use it before I returned. I placed another towel in a cardboard box and put a wire cake tray in readiness to cover the top. As I unwrapped the swift I had a quick glance at it, and wondered whether it was the male or the female which had been temporarily relieved of the duties of feeding the young. I placed the bird inside the box and put it on a stool next to the oven so that the warm air from the kitchen would dry its feathers.

After lunch was over, I saw that the plumage was drier but still very dishevelled, though the bird was looking much brighter. I wondered how I could help to straighten the feathers. The bird would not preen itself in so unnatural a situation, and it could not be released until its plumage was neat and straight. Then I remembered a soft baby's hairbrush I once had, and searching around, found it to be the very thing I needed. I took the swift on my hand and gently brushed its back and breast. Finally I opened out each long tapered wing and stroked it towards the tips.

I marvelled to think that those very wings I opened in my hands had carried the bird to vast heights and up to sixty miles an hour for thousands of miles on migration. What a superbly designed creature! Other than for fighting, mating and clinging to the nest entrance, its tiny legs are seldom used and certainly not for landing on the ground, since the swift with its long wings is usually unable to take off from a flat surface. The minute soft beak serves little purpose in itself; when catching its food in flight, the swift does not, as most people imagine, fly with mouth open scooping in insects, but, according to David Lack, darts about the skies selecting its prey.

I arranged the feathers on my bird as well as I could and hoped that the rain would soon stop before, as I then thought, the swift became weak for lack of food and before its young in the nest started to suffer.

By four o'clock the rain had ceased and the clouds lifted, so the time had come to bid farewell to this remarkable bird. Though no swifts, swallows or house martins were about the sky, I took it into the garden and decided to release it. I threw it up into the air and was delighted and relieved to see its wings open. With a fast, powerful flight it circled the area and was shortly joined by another swift—possibly its mate—and after several seconds others appeared from nowhere until the parent from the nest was no longer recognizable in the circling throng. Away it flew on its fly-catching mission, and I felt grateful to have been given the opportunity to see, at close quarters, such an unusual and extraordinary creature.

2

Tawny Owls in My Life

As I grew older my childhood interest in wild creatures increased and I became concerned, where animals or birds were injured and left to fend for themselves, or where anything wild was kept in captivity, to do all I could to return them to the freedom of the wild. I was encouraged by some successes in rearing abandoned youngsters and in nursing injured creatures back to health to take on more and more of this work. At first I dealt only with casualties I found myself. Gradually, as people got to know of my concern for the injured wild, all sorts of cases came my way.

June is the time that my house and garden becomes a temporary orphanage for many homeless creatures. Over the last four years, in response to dozens of calls for help by letter and telephone, I have nursed seven badgers, three foxes, four hedgehogs, thirty-nine tawny owls, forty-six barn owls, two short-eared owls, one long-eared owl, six little owls (that is all of the five species of owls breeding in Britain), as well as eight sparrow-hawks, two buzzards, sundry waders and passerines and more than forty kestrels.

It was a hen sparrow-hawk, a beautiful creature with piercing golden eyes but quite unable to fly, that led to my rearing one of the most absorbing tawny owls I have ever nursed. The sparrow-hawk had been shot in the wing, and tissue had grown over the injury, affecting the joint far more than the initial wound. An operation was unavoidable. It so happened that Brian Coles, my veterinary surgeon, was at that time caring for an attractive young tawny owl not long out of the nest which had been found exhausted in Bebington. The old yew trees in the cemetery there have provided a home for tawny owls for many years but this young owlet had become parted from its parents and flown in amongst the houses and shops. Exhausted and unable to return to the trees by daybreak, it had taken refuge in a shop doorway. In exchange for my vet's operation on the sparrow-hawk I agreed to take over the tawny owl, to rear it and prepare it for the wild.

At that time, diurnal residents occupied my small aviary, so I prepared the large summerhouse as a temporary shelter for this distinguished guest. I leaned an old ladder against one wall and placed branches of ash across the other side near to the open, wire-netting covered window. The glazed south-facing front of the summerhouse was draped with curtains to keep the interior cool on sunny days, and to prevent the bird from injuring itself against the glass.

Both sexes of tawny owl have identical plumage which makes them impossible to differentiate, but I called this one 'he'. Very soon after his release from his small carrying basket he began to feel at home in the summerhouse. The name for my owl which came first to mind (and somehow automatically) was 'Hooter', after the tawny owl owned by the naturalist and author, the late Miss Frances Pitt. I had the privilege of seeing and studying the original Hooter and I hoped very much that my little Hooter, at present covered in juvenile plumage, would grow into as fine a creature as his namesake.

From the first I was determined to feed him on as much natural food as possible, so, with the help of friends, I collected and fed him on woodmice, voles, sparrows, pigeons, young rabbits and other small mammals found dead on the road. At that time I had three predators, a badger, a sparrow-hawk and a tawny owl, all needing similar food. This made a deep-freeze a necessity during the hot summer days. The proprietary vitamin Adexolin was the only additive that I used, but it ensured that all young animals thrived.

I gave Hooter a dead mouse for his first supper and watched his eating method with fascination. I later found that live food is essential for owls and that he followed the same procedure whether the mouse was alive or dead. When it was offered to him on his feeding platform, he would raise his wings and pounce onto the mouse, gripping it with his claws. Crouching over it, he would nibble along the tail and hind legs with his sharp beak and then, turning it round in his talons, do the same all over the body up to the head, as though tenderizing it before eating it. To eat he would always begin with the head and, striking deftly with his beak, he would pluck off pieces and swallow them with closed eyes, as though enjoying each morsel to the full. One lump after another was pulled from his kill in this way, and each was consumed with the same expression of delight until he had reached just below the front legs of the mouse. Then, without pausing he would stop his plucking and swallow the remainder whole in two or three gulps until the last small tip of the tail had disappeared inside.

On his third day in the summerhouse Hooter regurgitated his first pellet, a good sign of health that was almost as exciting as seeing an egg being laid. Although I had collected various pellets in the wild, this was the first actual delivery I had witnessed. As I entered the door Hooter made a noisy clacking with his tongue from his perch on the top rung of the ladder. My experience with his namesake told me that this indicated displeasure or discomfort before disgorging a pellet of the bones and fur of some previously eaten animal. While gathering up the soiled newspapers covering the floor under his roosting places, I talked softly to him as he watched my movements. Suddenly he stood up very straight and spread his wings, and then ejected from his mouth a large grey pellet about two inches long and half an inch thick. It dropped with a dull thud onto the floor. Then, settling down once more into a comfortable and fluffed-up position on his ladder, his upper eyelids began to lift up and down over his large black eyes and, snuggling down on one foot with the other pulled up under him, he fell asleep. On another day he scratched his beak rapidly with his foot and ejected a pellet, as though using his claw to help the removal.

I refer to Hooter as having a mouth rather than a beak because the owl's beak, like the swift's, is small for the size of its head. But when an owl is swallowing a large mouse whole, his face seems literally to open up like a frog's and the mouth stretches across from under one eye disc to the other, the small beak appearing as a tiny 'nose' in the centre. Owls are bifocal (both eyes facing the front) with a beak like a small nose with coarse hairs at each side, and they have the face of a weird mammal rather than a bird. Their ears are located at the outer rim of the eye disc and open up distinctly as night falls, when their keen hearing is put to full use. Unlike the passerine birds which perch with three toes to the front and one to the rear, it is interesting to note that from under the owl's long fluffy skirt of buff and brown, his feathered legs terminate in two large claws, front and rear.

When Hooter was still quite small I thought it a good idea to fit leather jesses on him, to enable me to handle him more easily. These were simply made from a six-inch by half-inch strip of soft leather, with a small slit in one end. The other end was threaded through the slit and the leg slipped through the loop which was then drawn up neatly round his leg. He showed little objection to the jesses, and flew about as though he had no attachments, but in the morning he would always be roosting peacefully on his ladder, with the jesses lying undamaged on the floor!

I decided to watch and see what this little Houdini did to free his legs from their restriction. Amazingly, the wise young bird, without any fuss or bother, lifted one foot and carefully gripped the correct piece close round his leg with his beak, and slowly pulled it upwards until the long end slipped through the slot into which it was threaded. With a slight shake of his fluffy head he dropped the leather to the floor, and repeated the process with the other leg. Clearly he was the cleverer creature and I did not try jesses again; but simply slipped my gloved fingers under his toes when I wanted to hold him. As he preferred things this way, he would oblige by stepping onto my hand to be moved. To hold an owl round the body with its wings down like a small bird is like holding a sponge. There is nothing firm on which to grip and the owl is likely to draw its wings out and flap them wildly.

On several occasions while I reared Hooter I was awakened at dawn by the loud, prolonged and anxious clucking of my pair of blackbirds dancing about on the lawn in front of the summerhouse and because, in summer, this used to happen soon after 4 a.m., I took a poor view of being forced out of bed at this hour. At first I thought it must be the magpie threatening the blackbird's nest in the hedge. When I investigated there was no magpie in sight, though there was a stray cat sitting on top of the ten foot hawthorn hedge. But this did not seem to be the cause of the blackbirds' anxiety, as their cries continued long after I had chased the marauder away. On searching closely I noticed that the curtains in the summerhouse had been drawn back and, sitting on the floor, peering out of the window, was my small fluffy owl, completely motionless and unperturbed. The blackbirds had seen him looking out and instinct must have told them that he was a predator and should be driven away at all cost.

This alarm signal by the blackbirds happened regularly and I was forced to slip out in my nightdress, half asleep, and simply wave little Hooter up onto his ladder, drawing the curtains together again, as much as to say, 'Go to bed and sleep now that it is dawn, and stop annoying those little ruffians at the door'. I am sure in the end that it was the blackbirds who actually baited him to come to the window, to tease and scold him, impassive though he remained!

Time passed and Hooter began to shed his beautiful soft down. Every day the floor became more and more covered with fluffy breast feathers, which wafted about when he flew from perch to perch. His adult plumage grew apace until much of his time was spent preening. This he did by running his strong hooked beak down the length of each feather to remove the grey quill-like protection. Much stronger feathers, with bolder markings forming vertical bars, wider and darker in colour, replaced the fine gossamer horizontal brown bars on the breast. His soft fawn head feathers were superseded by new plumage which formed a coronet-like marking above the beak and eye discs, while his primary wing feathers grew dark brown and strong. During the day, while roosting, his eyes were completely shut, so that only the feathered discs were visible. But, as night began to fall, he would wake up and, in his one-sided manner, stretch one leg and one wing downwards on the same side of his body, revealing the tremendous size of his shapely wings when fully extended. Often he would fly down onto the floor where a large bowl of water awaited him for his bath. Owls are attracted to water, and he would stand in about four inches

Hooter after a bathe; and eating a mouse

Wildone perching at night

Rusty and Dusky

of it, before jumping onto the floor, splashing and shaking the water all over the place. Then he would fly (if he could) onto a perch to preen himself. If too bedraggled and wet, he waddled into a corner looking as pathetic as something that the cat brought in.

The time had now come to teach him to catch and kill mice for himself, and to learn that food was to be found on the ground and not always on the top of his feeding box. I began his training by tying a strand of cotton to the hind leg of a dead mouse and putting it on the floor, moving the mouse slightly to attract his attention. In the beginning he would only react to the moving mouse if it was a few inches away. Gradually I increased the distance until he could spot the mouse even while he sat high up on the top of the ladder. Then he would hop lower and lower and finally pounce the last short distance directly onto the dead animal. There he would crouch over his prey, clutching it in his claws, wings spread in a guarding posture and head held forward. While he was in this position I would cut the cotton and he would fly up to his eating perch to dissect his 'kill' or to eat it whole.

He became so adept at catching mice in this way, eventually pouncing direct from the top of the ladder, that I produced a live mouse caught in the hedgerow in a Longworth cage trap. It was a mistake to offer him this woodmouse (*Apodemus sylvaticus*) as the first live animal, for these little creatures are extremely lively and can both run and jump at a tremendous speed. I left the mouse in the summerhouse with him for the night, thinking that he would have dealt with it by morning. I was in for a surprise. By the morning the mouse had taken up residence and had made itself at home, constructing a nest of newspaper in a corner on the floor.

I left it there expecting that its life would not be long. Although it seemed to have dissected the owl's pellets in search of nourishment I thought that food would be the main problem. After a week had passed and the mouse was as lively as ever, I guessed there must be some secret to its longevity. I observed that all the owl's food for the night—two day-old chicks (reject chicks purchased dead from a hatchery)—had gone from the top of his cage, and it seemed to me that the owl preferred this food to the mouse which shared his home. But when I cleaned out the torn newspapers and the fallen juvenile feathers which covered the floor I was amazed to find the two dead chicks by the mouse's nest. The bold little mouse which was supposed to be food for the owl was climbing to the top of the owl cage and dragging the owl's food back to its nest. If anyone was starving it was Hooter!

Something had to be done about this absurd situation, so I set to work to try and catch the mouse and pitch it outside. Life was far to cosy in the confines of the owl's territory, and this state of affairs simply had to be ended. Never thinking of the Longworth cage trap, I tried to catch the mouse by hand. Up the curtains it ran, and backwards and forwards along the rail. As I was about to close my hands around it, it sprang onto my shoulder, but instead of jumping onto the floor it proceeded to run about all over my back. I was unable to see it, and could only feel its delicate little feet travelling up and down my spine. Finally I shook it to the floor, the owl watching all the time from the top rung of his ladder. I was about to give up the chase when I saw the mouse starting to climb up one side of the ladder. To my amazement the sandy little creature with its large round ears, black beady eyes and long tail, continued ascending under the full gaze of the owl up to the top and onto its rung. There it sat washing its face within two inches of its arch-enemy. Hooter just sat there too, swinging his head from side to side as he stared at it, but making no further move. Then the mouse seemed to realise it could get no further and crept back to the side of the ladder and slid all the way back to the floor.

Within an hour it was safely inside the small cage trap, but I decided that as it was a mouse of such spirit and character I would release it in the hedgerow.

After that Hooter's live offerings came in the form of voles or white mice, both somewhat slower in movement than wood-mice. Hooter certainly knew what to do with them. When I released them on the floor they hardly ran three feet before the owl would drop down from his perch with a thud, straight onto his small victims, gripping them tightly with his claws until they were dead.

Now the time had come to take him into the old stone barn in the oak woods. The barn had a wire netting door and in this way I could introduce him to the sight and sounds of the area in which he would eventually be released. In the barn he could fly from one perch to the next and could hear the calls of the native tawny owls in the trees outside.

Just one week after his transfer to the barn, on a fine warm evening, I began the final stage of his return to the wild. After going inside to see him and talk to him for the last time, I placed his nightly meal of two dead woodmice on the floor in the open doorway. He knew his name now and he responded to my quiet words with a slow blink of his large eyes and a soft cooing sound. When I knew that he had seen his mice I retired.

The sun had gone down behind the hills across the lake and the midges were out in force as I sat quietly in the long grass and bracken, waiting with my back to the trees. I had long anticipated this moment when I would witness his flight to freedom from the shelter of the home I had provided for the last few months.

Silently moving towards the door, he stood, head bent forward, peering out to see the world beyond before venturing forth. He made one or two flights to the back of the barn, then flew forward once more before finally, noiselessly, with wings stretched to full length, he passed through the opening and landed on a tussock of grass in front of me, just outside the shelter of his barn.

Although he had seemed very large in his previous home, out in the open he looked small. For fifteen minutes or more he stood, his dark ear slots spread open wide to catch the many sounds around him, turning his head not only from side to side but up and over until only his throat was visible, so that he could see in every direction.

On a summer evening, dusk is often heralded in the woods by several minutes of total silence, when the breeze drops to a complete calm, the birds cease their singing and not a sound is heard. Then slowly the leaf litter on the woodland floor starts to crackle and come alive with the feet of small creatures, like the sound of pattering raindrops on dry leaves.

In the grass in front of him, Hooter detected the movement of a small beetle and after stretching himself to his full height, he arched his neck so as to look down and see what strange creature moved so close. He was doubtful and took two steps backwards from the sound, jerking his head this way and that, trying to locate the movement. The minute insect must have vanished into the soil, for he turned his head upwards and searched the skies for other life. Then I saw his gaze fix upon the movement of a pipistrelle bat, which came from the colony roosting in the roof of our cottage, flitting in the dusk of the evening, amongst the large trees. His eyes and ears were trained upon it, following it through the gloom and into the darkness of the trees which overhung his barn.

Quite suddenly he spread his soft pale wings and wafted silently up into the branches of a hazel tree. He must have missed his footing. The movement of the leaves marked his fall to the rocky floor below. But soon he was up again, passing in the darkness like a large moth in the night, and landing on a rock on the hillside behind his barn.

The silent flight of owls has evolved primarily to enable them to hear their prey, unhampered by the sound of their own movement. No doubt it also prevents the prey itself from hearing its enemy. A tawny owl's ears can detect higher frequencies than ours, and they can distinguish the high-pitched sound of a vole and other small mammals from the low tone of rain or wind on a stormy night.

The last I saw of Hooter that first night, when it was almost dark, was as a silent ghostly form moving higher and higher into the tall branches of a sycamore tree. I bade him farewell and strolled back to the cottage close by. The final call I heard, as he perched in his tree, was in answer to the loud 'ke-wick ke-wick' of an adult owl which had approached unheard from the opposite direction. A duet of 'ke-wick's and 'whoo-oo's continued until the two birds faded away into the depths of the oak woods and the dark night.

Weeks passed and I would listen to the sounds of the different owls hooting around the cottage, one of which I thought could possibly be Hooter because of his husky sounding 'whoo-oo' common among juvenile tawny owls. I was never certain of this until one still dark night in September, when I was walking among the oak trees in the dim light thrown by the light at the rear of the cottage. From a low branch of a nearby tree came a very loud 'kewick' repeated many times, so close as to be almost deafening. By the light of my torch I could see a round and fluffy shape perched some ten feet up the tree about twenty feet away. I held the bird in the beam of light, and as I crept closer he turned and faced me, jerking his head from side to side. I recognized his soft breast feathers and quietly called 'Hooter, whoo-oo' until I was standing within eight feet of the tree, and he seemed to be just above my head. We stared at each other for several seconds, then he raised his massive downy wings and, turning his body, drifted noiselessly away into the depths of the dark wood and out of range of the torch. How rewarding it was to know for certain that after several weeks he was still around the cottage, had found his place with the other owls, and was able to find his own food in woodland and pasture.

The months passed, and autumn turned to winter. The trees became golden and then bare, the fine tracery of their branches silhouetted against the clear Christmas moon. I was preparing for the great festival with my family around me, when, instead of carols on the night air, the clear strong voice of my owl came once more from a tree beside the cottage, calling me outside with his welcoming greeting. It was six months after his flight to freedom, and I had not heard his call for a long time. Joyfully I went outside and, with torch in hand, saw him standing high up in the branches of an oak tree, large and pale against the darkness, looking down at me, and calling as he had done before. Replying to his calls, I talked to him as I drew nearer and nearer to the base of the tree until I stood immediately below it. He craned his head down to look at me, watching my every movement. After about fifteen minutes I moved further up into the quiet woods. To my surprise, Hooter ceased his calling and floated on outstretched wings between the trees, every now and then resting for a few seconds on a branch beside me. After a few words with him, he followed again as I quietly trod the leafy tracks made by the feet of passing deer.

I went back to the cottage and into the light, pausing for a final farewell to Hooter who had returned to his nearby tree beside the garden wall. His loud calls continued for a few minutes until he turned his head away from me and, spreading his three-foot wings, disappeared into the night.

Again that autumn I was given two other owls of the same age whom I called Brown Owl and Grey Owl. They had been fed entirely on an artificial diet. We kept them all winter in the large new aviary which we had constructed in the garden beside the wood. On their own, unable to hunt well enough to catch the sparse winter mouse population, they would not have survived.

March came and after the usual hunting lessons I released the two owls to join my Hooter, who showed immediate interest. In fact, he showed so much interest that once, on a rough wet night, he broke in through the wire roof of the aviary and joined Brown and Grey Owl in their shelter. When I found him there next morning I made a close inspection and had a few words with him. Then I opened the door and let him fly out into the sunlit woods.

A year previously I had fixed an owl nesting box to the under-side of a north-facing bough of a sycamore tree. It was a three foot long by eight inches square wooden tube. When I checked this in early spring I removed the remains of a jackdaw's nest and covered the base with sawdust. To my delight two weeks later a 'ke-wicking' was heard from the nest box indicating that some owl was interested in it.

I was away from home for a time, and when I returned early in June I went immediately to the owl tree. It was dusk, and I saw my familiar rufus Brown Owl fly out. But what was even more exciting, I heard the hissing of young from the depths of the box. Brown Owl was promptly joined by the handsome and immaculate Hooter from his roosting place high in an adjoining oak tree, and I was able to observe that Hooter, released the previous June, and Brown Owl, released that March, were the father and mother of the young owlets in my nesting box. I felt that this was a one hundred per cent conservation success and it gave me a real thrill of achievement. I had reared both parents separately, I had built a suitable nest site for them to rear their young, out in the wild, free from all restraint, and a couple of young owlets had been added to the population of British birds of prey. How I wished that I could have the chance to do the same with the rare barn owl!

Day and night the parents fed the young, and much commotion was caused during daylight hours amongst the vociferous jays and pinking blackbirds when the owls flew in and out of the box with food. Occasionally they sat in the sunshine conspicuous on an old tree stump, watching for mouse movements in the grass.

Towards dusk, the young, still oatmeal-coloured, climbed up the steep floor of the nest box and peeped out, gazing at the outside world of the woods. Occasionally, with a shake of the head, they would disgorge a large warm pellet, which would fall with a thud thirty feet to the ground below. Day by day they grew bolder and, with much preening and stretching, on 2 July Wildone and Wildtwo dropped from the box and with large outspread wings flew into a nearby yew tree.

In March, when I had released Grey Owl and Brown Owl, the local R.S.P.C.A. Inspector, Tony Crittenden, had rescued two very young owlets which had been stolen from a nest. He gave them to me to rear. By a coincidence these two owlets became a brown and a grey, and I called them Rusty and Dusky. I kept them in the warmth of the cottage, and reared them in a box containing cotton wool covered with tissues, laid over a hot-water bottle. When I first received these two owlets they were so frail that I fed them on raw egg and glucose, but as they grew stronger they eagerly ate pieces of mouse, offered on the end of tweezers. They made excellent progress, their white down changing to oatmeal, while their primary feathers grew, shaping their tiny useless wings into large strong ones. By now they were exercising their legs and claws by clambering about in the box, and they stretched their wings as they sat on a towel spread on the bench. The owls were watched over by our beagle, who every now and then pushed his nose into their soft feathers, performing his customary role of guardian to all wild creatures who came into our household.

At about the age when young owls leave the nest, they were transferred to the aviary. They now looked more like owlets and they gave their hissing call every time I approached. Occasionally, when they were five weeks old, I took them out into the woods and watched them trying out their wings as they fluttered about between the rocks and low branches. Until they could fend for themselves I carried them falcon-wise on my hands back to the aviary.

Now at dusk the evening air resounded with the food call of four young owls, Rusty and Dusky in the aviary and Wildone and Wildtwo in the nest box. There was also the powerful 'ke-wick' and 'whoo-oo' of the adults, Hooter and Brown Owl, as they scoured the area for mice and voles amongst the dry leaves and rocks of the woodland.

Rusty and Dusky were now learning to catch live mice in preparation for the return to the wild. Training owls to catch live prey is essential to their survival, and with so many owls to feed I began to breed my own dark-coloured mice. Trapping live mice in the wild would only deprive other wildlife of its natural food.

At about this time I noticed that Hooter and Brown Owl were leaving Wildone and Wildtwo to hunt for themselves much more. These two owls took to calling loudly just outside the aviary, where they could see the food put down for Rusty and Dusky. In fact it seemed as though the orphans invited them to the enclosure, because they moved over to the woodland side of the aviary, watching and calling loudly when they heard the 'tsicking' of Wildone and Wildtwo in the distance. They behaved towards them in a manner of complete acceptance.

On 13 August I rolled back the aviary roof and released Rusty and Dusky, who flew with powerful wing beats to the top branches of some tall trees. The four young owls made a terrific commotion. All the owls' voices were quite different in sound and tone, in huskiness and intensity. After much jostling and calling Rusty and Dusky departed to take up residence in another part of the wood, leaving Wildone and Wildtwo in possession of the home territory.

At dusk the following night I strolled very slowly and quietly in search of Rusty and Dusky in their new territory. The daylight was fading rapidly, no wind stirred the leaves, and as darkness fell the whole world became silent and still. I hardly dared move for fear of breaking that silence. But as always, the leafy floor gradually stirred into a continuous faint sound of clicking and rustling as small insects, beetles, toads and wood-mice crept from their daytime slumber.

The husky rasping 'whoo-oo' of Wildone came from a distant tree, and soon he floated on silent wings over towards the stone barn, where he settled high in the leafy canopy of an oak. I knew my orphans were in the wood somewhere, and that if I called their names I was sure they would answer with their soft voices, as they always had done. But the summer night was so very quiet that I felt, however soft my call, it would break the stillness. When I dared to whisper 'Rusty', 'Dusky', I not only surprised myself by my own voice, but the woodland came alive with the noise of small hooves rattling down the bank in front of me. I stood beside a tree and felt as though the creatures of the oakwoods were closing in on me as the sound of hooves came nearer and then stopped amongst the bracken and rocks above the deer track on which I was walking. Again they came nearer, then stopped, and nearer again, until I could hear the sniff of their nostrils as two young roe deer raised their heads and tried to catch my scent in the soft evening air. I could see little except the silhouettes of ferns, and amongst them an occasional movement of the head and ears of the suspicious roe deer creeping up to get a whiff of the strange creature sharing their woodland hillside. I raised my binoculars to see them better in the dusk, but they melted away into the gloom.

Wildone and his sister Wildtwo had passed through the trees and flown out of earshot, but the clicking and crackling of life among the leaf litter was now accompanied by the almost in-audible soft cooing of Dusky and Rusty, reassuring me that they would shortly start their search for food along the woodland floor. But although I often heard their distinctive voices I never saw Rusty and Dusky again. I missed the cooing which used to greet me when I approached the aviary during their daytime roosting. But they were now fully feathered, handsome adult birds of prey, out on the serious business of hunting to live.

At two o'clock one night Wildone was making so much noise with his hungry call that I got out of bed, took a joint of rabbit from the refrigerator, and put it on the aviary roof. Immediately he was down, seizing it in his claws and flew away to eat it on a branch in the woods.

But having once found that I would satisfy their hungry call Wildone and Wildtwo grew more demanding. Each evening at dusk I would see on the stark white branches of the trees beside our cottage their ghostly owlish shapes waiting hopefully for bits of mice and rabbit to be put out for them on the lawn. They used to haunt me like this, and, although still responding to the call of their parents, would drop down for the extra tasty morsels that I put out for them, returning to eat in the seclusion of the woods.

Gradually the calls of the parents—Hooter and Brown Owl —became less frequent, and Wildtwo appeared more rarely. Wildone, now fully grown and hunting for himself, remained as master of the area, still visiting the garden to take from the grass any food that I might offer.

In March the following year Tony Crittenden brought me another owl. It was an adult tawny owl, which I called Owleight. It was suffering from a double fracture of the ulna of the right wing and it looked very hunched and dejected. As the radius was virtually splinting the ulna, my veterinary surgeon decided not to pin the fracture but suggested that I should keep her in close confinement in my hospital cage. This would prevent her from making any movement other than when preening. The box cage, which had a wire mesh door, had smooth wooden sides with no protruberances on which the bird might injure herself. Owleight was confined for four weeks and fed on rabbit, chicks and pigeon, always complete with bones, fur and feathers, and with added vitamins. She had a bowl of water in case she felt like bathing. Under her perch was a tray of sawdust to make it easy to clean the cage. All birds and mammals taken from the wild when mature are difficult in captivity, and one has to gain their confidence before they will start to thrive. Care must be taken when one approaches or cleans out the cage to prevent the sudden movement which causes the bird to flush.

Rather than putting the nursing cage in some quiet place (on first thought the natural thing to do with a frightened bird), I placed it in a prominent position in the kitchen, the busiest room in my cottage. Gradually the bird became used to seeing me moving about all the time and as I caused it no distress it accepted the situation quite quickly. Had Owleight been put in a quiet corner away from everyday life she would have flushed every time anybody went near her and this might well have caused her further injury.

After about a week in the cage in the kitchen, the owl became quite used to life there. She was so much at ease that one morning I found the water from her bowl splashed all over the cage, and the floor in front awash. Owleight herself looked in far better condition, having bathed and preened herself, and I now had great hopes for her recovery. Eating well, she re-gurgitated pellets daily, and was looking quite a different bird.

A month passed and I took her once more down to my vet's surgery, where he anaesthetized and X-rayed her to see whether the wing had healed. To my delight the X-ray showed complete success. Now she could go into the large aviary to strengthen her muscles and weather her plumage to make it capable of withstanding all seasons before I released her.

The day she was transferred, 5 April, was very rough and windy with rain, hail and snow. I hesitated to put her out in the aviary after living in the artificial warmth of the kitchen, but as the aviary had an excellent sheltered area, I decided she was better outside. Her wings were weak but she managed to get to the higher perches by scrambling up the netting and soon stood aloft scanning the world outside, raking her head from side to side, in her typical quizzical manner.

At dawn on the third day I woke to hear her calling, accompanied by the wild owls in the woods, and at dusk Wildone and his mate came down to the aviary or stood on top of the dry stone wall between the aviary and the woods. There were some very noisy fights through the netting between Wildone's mate and Owleight. Eventually Wildone chased off his mate and returned to perch on top of the aviary, talking to Owleight within.

At 8 o'clock next morning Wildone was roosting on top of the aviary, peering down at the captive Owleight, whilst she stood as close as she could to him, divided only by the netting. Both owls were extremely friendly, so I concluded that Wildone

39

was a male and Owleight a female. At 11 a.m. Wildone was dive-bombed and mobbed by jackdaws, blackbirds and a mistlethrush, and was forced to leave the aviary roof. The bushes just over the wall were alive with bluetits, a robin, chaffinches and other small birds voicing their protest at the two intruders. Wildone took refuge high in a sycamore tree and Owleight, after clambering on the netting walls in her attempt to follow, eventually retired to the covered area of the aviary.

Wildone continued to visit each evening. Meanwhile Owleight's flight became stronger, and at night she became as vociferous as all the other owls in the woods. By 12 April she was fit and well. Her plumage was magnificent, with dark markings on her breast feathers forming a distinct chevron design down her front. At dusk I rolled back the roof of the aviary. Instantly the captive Owleight flew from her roost under cover, to a perch at the top of the aviary. Pausing for only a few seconds, she passed straight out and away up through the trees to the highest branch about a hundred yards off. Her colour was very dark and I soon lost sight of her in the dusk. There was unbelievable power in those wings only so recently broken and useless.

Out in the woods with my tape recorder I made a recording of the owl calls as she and Wildone greeted each other, to the accompaniment of the other wild owls there. There were no sounds of fighting, so Wildone's mate must have left the territory.

A week after Owleight's release I put down five dark-coloured mice on the woodland floor. Her calling started soon afterwards and within half an hour my ex-patient flew down on her soft wings, paused a few seconds and then rose again, large and majestic with a mouse in her claws.

After the departure of all my owls in late August, I took any surplus mice from my breeding scheme and released them in suitable territory in the oak woods. The mice, in helping to build up the wild stock for the winter, would provide food for owls during the hard weather and, being a native strain, they stood a good chance of survival.

My idea that mice would enjoy life in the woods was not shared by the mice themselves, for one evening in November as I was getting my wellingtons out of the cupboard in the utility room, a mouse shot out under my feet. I was even more surprised when I realized it was one of my own mice. It had travelled across as much as half a mile of wild territory to the very shelf where its breeding enclosure had been fitted. Eventually all of the eleven mice that I had released into the wild returned to the safety of the box where they were born.

Little has been known or recorded about the homing instincts of mice, but they seem to be able to find their way back over relatively large distances on unfamiliar ground. I have had many instances of similar behaviour since then.

My hopes that the owl box out in the woods would be used by Owleight and Wildone were dashed when, in spite of several attempts by other owls, it was occupied by jackdaws. After modifying the box with a lid which was closed in the daytime and opened at dusk, the jackdaws were kept out during the breeding season.

I was delighted when, after nine months in the wild, Wildone and Owleight took over the box and laid their first eggs some time in the following March. My husband and I watched and listened hopefully, and in spite of the jackdaws (who attempted to build their nest on top of the sitting owl by pushing sticks down into the box) the first quiet hissings of two young owlets were heard on 27 April. Wildthree and Wildfour had hatched out. I was away a good deal after that, and so I saw little of the young owls, but on 27 May the familiar calling of young owlets was heard in the woods and after a search I found two fluffy youngsters roosting in the nearby trees. They had left the box the previous night, and I saw the superbly marked Owleight feeding them.

Both the young owls gradually moved away from the nest area, as they followed their parents in their search for food. In the still twilight of summer, when the moon was rising and almost full, I last saw this family of owls feeding under the leafy cover of the oak woods. The two fluffy oatmeal-coloured balls were sitting high in the branches hissing their hungry calls to their parents. The elder of the two fledglings uttered a low note while the younger made a slightly higher call. The large dark form of the female, Owleight, glided noiselessly backwards and forwards through the trees, silhouetted against the fading light uttering her quiet, soft, 'wit-wit-wit' to her youngsters. As she approached, their voices quickened and strained to a crescendo, one high and one low on their different notes, becoming louder and faster. Owleight landed on a branch beside them, rested for a second and then passed them the food, while they trembled their large wings. Finally she spread her dark form and drifted away into the woods in search of insects and the occasional mouse.

Once more my hand-reared and injured owls had bred successfully and reared their young in the nest box I had provided for them. The owl family tree on page 43 shows clearly how these many owls fit into the nest-box breeding picture.

According to John Sparks and Tony Soper in their book, *Owls*, young owlets in the wild face great hazards. Once they fly from the nest they must learn to hunt for themselves and become efficient killers, although the parent birds continue to provide their offspring with the bulk of their food until October or November. Occasionally, if hunting is difficult and the tawny owls have had a clutch of three or possibly even four young, they may give up the struggle of feeding them earlier than usual, and leave the young to chance, in which case they seldom survive.

Even under normal circumstances, life is hard for young owlets at the onset of autumn and winter, for already the older and more experienced owls resident in the area will drive off the young to a vacant place of woodland. This happens frequently in our oak woods, and as I wander through the woods I can observe the different owls I have reared and see into which vacant niches they have been driven. Having been fed and trained to catch their own food, they are already more powerful than the young of the wild, and are able to defend the territory into which they have moved. But if there is no such area over which they can show their dominance, as the weather becomes colder and the rodent population declines, the young and inexperienced owls competing for food will be the first to succumb to cold and starvation. A pair of tawny owls will lay from two to four eggs in one year, but possibly only one will survive. Once the second summer is attained a young owl's chances are

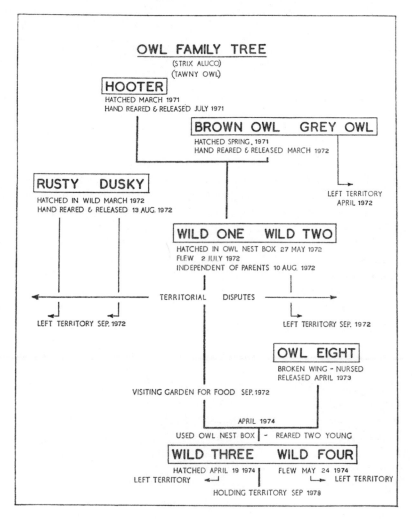

OWL FAMILY TREE
(STRIX ALUCO)
(TAWNY OWL)

HOOTER
HATCHED MARCH 1971
HAND REARED & RELEASED JULY 1971

BROWN OWL   GREY OWL
HATCHED SPRING, 1971
HAND REARED & RELEASED MARCH 1972

LEFT TERRITORY
APRIL 1972

RUSTY   DUSKY
HATCHED IN WILD MARCH 1972
HAND REARED & RELEASED 13 AUG. 1972

WILD ONE   WILD TWO
HATCHED IN OWL NEST BOX 27 MAY 1972
FLEW 2 JULY 1972
INDEPENDENT OF PARENTS 10 AUG. 1972

◄———————— TERRITORIAL   DISPUTES ————————►

LEFT TERRITORY SEP. 1972

LEFT TERRITORY SEP. 1972

OWL EIGHT
BROKEN WING - NURSED
RELEASED APRIL 1973

VISITING GARDEN FOR FOOD SEP. 1972

APRIL 1974
USED OWL NEST BOX | - REARED TWO YOUNG

WILD THREE   WILD FOUR
HATCHED APRIL 19 1974   FLEW MAY 24 1974
LEFT TERRITORY ◄—   —► LEFT TERRITORY
HOLDING TERRITORY SEP 1978

greatly increased, and in maturity the rate of mortality from natural causes decreases.

So there is much to be said for rearing and training young owls in captivity. At least when they go out into the wide world they will have been helped over the first hurdle: learning how to catch and kill efficiently to keep themselves alive.

3

Badgers through the Gate

Bodger, the first badger cub which I reared from a tiny orphaned cub, came my way as a result of a telephone call for
help. A farmer had found three cubs, injured, cold and weak
with hunger, and left to die after they had been dug out of
their nearby sett by badger diggers. The men had taken the
mother but, thinking that the cubs were too injured to sell,
abandoned them in the field. Two of the cubs died before I
could collect them and my little sow, Bodger, was not far from
death. It took several months to nurse, rear and prepare her
for life in the wild, but in the end she passed to the freedom
of the woodland and fellside with her natural setts around my
Lakeland home.

Ever since Bodger passed through her badger gate from
captivity to freedom — but, alas, to accidental death — many
others, like Baloo, Puffles, Buboo and Tiny-Toes, have by gentle
persuasion, taken a different route and now flourish in the
rocky, bracken-covered fellsides and lowland pastures of the
Lakeland countryside where I live.

All these badgers, casualties of man's inhumanity, were given
to me to rear and return to the wild like Bodger, the central
figure of my earlier book, *Through the Badger Gate*. Some were
pathetic little creatures when they reached me, often so badly
injured that they did not seem to care whether they lived or
died. Puffles, a boar of five weeks, was rescued from badger
diggers in South Wales, and he carried on his neck the scars
made by the sharp badger tongs of the hunters. These in-
struments of torture can still be purchased commercially,
and I keep a pair so that visitors can see and handle them,
feel the sharpness of their inter-locking teeth, and appreciate
the power that can be exerted on a badger's neck by the

forty-one inch handles when the tongs are closed together.

The use of tongs for pulling badgers from their setts, for holding badgers while terriers attack them, or for any other purpose connected with badgers, is now illegal, thanks to the Badgers Act of 1973. Puffles, for instance, had never been above ground, so he could in no way deserve such cruel treatment. But his suffering may have not been in vain, for such instances helped to convince Parliament of the need for protective legislation.

Gradually, as I nursed Puffles back to health, his injuries healed. For twelve weeks he was fed from a bottle, sleeping peacefully all the rest of the time like a young badger in the wild, where, suckled by its mother, it enjoys the warm dark comfort of its underground home until it is strong enough to forage for itself.

Puffles always lay on my knee to feed, his spoon-shaped tongue curled round the teat while his fore-paws pressed and kneaded the hand which held the bottle to his mouth. Even at this stage he lived in a wooden box (with a nine inch drainpipe as his only means of entry and exit) to give him the essential feeling of security he needed away from the sett. When I approached his box to feed him, as I did at frequent intervals throughout the day, he soon learnt to recognize the smell of the warm milk. His black and white face would peep out at the end of the drainpipe, his nose slightly raised to catch the welcome scent of food. Then, with a tiny yickering sound, he would stagger like a baby bear across to where I was sitting, and scrabble at my legs, asking to be lifted up on to my knee. There he would immediately roll himself onto his back in preparation for his feed, getting quite agitated if I did not instantly respond to his pleas. He was always hungry, and unless I quickly removed my hand would nip my finger in frustration as soon as the last drop had been taken from the bottle.

At twelve weeks old he progressed from straight Ostermilk No. 2 to a mixture of Farlene and Ostermilk, a more solid food which he took from the end of a spoon. At first this enraged him, as his instinct was to suckle long and vigorously if he could; but he was getting older and had to learn to accept his food from a dish. Next, minced raw meat was added to the

Farlene mixture, and this delighted his growing appetite until, at four months, milk was eliminated completely. He then progressed to puppy meal and minced meat, mixed with a little Bovril. A greedy youngster, at six months old he had grown both in size and strength, and the garage in which, after his evening romp and forage in the garden, he spent his nights, was turned into a complete shambles as a result of his inquisitive behaviour.

I hung a tyre and a broom to within a few inches of the floor from the roof of the garage to simulate his missing brothers and sisters. In play, he rolled and twisted through the tyre and tugged and wrestled with the brush, expending his abundant energy in this harmless and educational way. As it swung the heavy tyre buffeted him, and he gave out little growls and squeaks, just as he would have when playing with his natural family.

The strength and patience of Puffles quite amazed me. One morning I found the heavy, long-handled hydraulic jack in the garage fully extended. Fifteen up and down strokes are needed to lever it to this position, so either he had operated it at intervals during the course of the night, or had tackled it at one go, like one possessed. The former is the likelier explanation.

When he became completely nocturnal he was transferred to his Lakeland home: the artificial sett in the garden. Although I managed to contain him in his compound for a couple of nights, once he was introduced to the garden during the evening, no fencing I could provide could retain him after I had given him his supper. He was soon over the top of the netting, squeezing between the close strands of barbed wire, leaving large tufts of his hair on the barbs and coming down to the cottage door. The only alternative was to open the compound and give him the run of the garden all night. I went to bed, secretly pleading with him in thought, 'Stay in the garden this one night, for your safety, and tomorrow evening I will introduce you to the oakwoods through the badger gate.'

Next morning, there were signs of his grubbing for worms and leather-jackets in the grass. The carefully tended plants in the rockery had been uprooted where his strong snout, rooting down to the juicy grubs and eggs, had uncovered an ants' nest. But my relief was so great when I heard him safely asleep in

46

his bed of hay in the artificial sett, that I forgave the damage
to the rockery plants.

I did not want Puffles to enter the wide world from the
garden side of the cottage, so at dusk I introduced him straight-
away to the little gate in the drystone wall dividing his compound
from the rough and rocky ground in the oakwoods beyond. He
was such a boisterous, thrusting creature that he soon learnt to
push open the gate and go through, but once he had passed
beyond it he became much more cautious, for the unfamiliar
territory exhaled the strange scents of roe deer, rabbits and all
the other creatures of the woods.

Once I was over the wall and in the woods with him, his
confidence returned, and I strolled slowly while he found grubs
and insects hidden under stones and leaves. He returned frequently to the badger gate and became completely familiar
with its immediate surroundings before exploring deeper into
the woodland.

To avoid the pasture fields in which Bodger had met her
death, I led Puffles up through the woods, along the track
from the old stone barn to the platform made by the charcoal
burners hundreds of years ago. On we went, up and up through
the dark still night, through gaps in the old walls and across
woodland streams. Every now and again I stopped and watched
him rooting and exploring, until suddenly he would gallop
back to me, puffing like a little steam engine, rustling among
the dry leaves and twigs as he came. This was how he got his
name.

Often on these nightly expeditions my husband accompanied
me, and took photographs to record the young badger's behaviour. Sometimes progress was even slower than usual when
Puffles decided to melt into the darkness, as all badgers are
prone to do, plodding off on his own in quite a different direction from the one in which I was leading him. To hurry things
up my husband would then retrieve him and carry him back
over the rough ground to where I stood. On one such occasion,
he tripped over a half buried tree stump in the darkness and
the badger landed with a thump on the ground in front of
him. I visualized a worried and angry badger treating my
husband to a nasty nip; but no, Puffles simply stood there

47

waiting for his porter to regain his feet and lift him up again, to be carried back like a baby! Later when he made off up the steep craggy hillside through the trees, we ignored him, strolling on up to the far edge of the woods, across the lane and into the fields spread out at the foot of the mountains.

Here we had to cross a boggy patch by a small log bridge. But Puffles refused to go over. Instead he chose to make a detour along the illuminated drive of a warden's cottage, which enabled the occupants to watch his passage to the pastures. On this particular occasion, when he was left behind down in the woods, we waited at the field gate in the hope that he would follow our scent and catch up with us. Down the woodland track came the rustles and puffing of Puffles as he picked up our scent, and then his little striped face appeared round the corner of the wall as he emerged from the wood onto the lane where we were waiting. Before crossing, he musked at the base of the wall corner to mark his return, trotted across and musked on the other side. Then he joined us with much purring, as though indicating that we could now move on into the fields.

The walk from the badger gate in the garden to these fields used to take almost two hours, during which time we often passed a number of roe deer, who made their presence known by barking as they hurried off, startling us all. Sometimes Puffles was too afraid to continue our stroll, and galloped all the way home to the security of his sett. Occasionally we encouraged him to return to the woods by quietly reassuring him as we walked.

I felt confident, having led him a few times along the route, that he would use it when alone at night, and it was with great joy that I found his footprints in the mud near the log bridge long after he had become independent and returned to the wild.

Baloo, the most charming little sow I could have wished for, was my seventh badger. Like Bodger, my other sow, she was much quieter and gentler than the boars and a model of good behaviour. She followed my routine and made a perfect return to the wild.

After Puffles passed to freedom and before Baloo came my

way, a dead badger was picked up on a farm in Gloucestershire and a post-mortem examination revealed that bovine tuberculosis was the cause of death. For some years local farmers and the Ministry of Agriculture had been concerned at the persistent recurrence of tuberculosis in the cattle in the area, and many people thought that badgers were the carriers of the disease.

Two other localized areas of tuberculosis in cattle were known to exist in Cornwall and Wiltshire, so a study was made of the badgers in those areas. While there is absolutely no doubt that badgers can receive the bacillus from infected cattle (from their habit of turning up cowpats in the pasture fields in search of dor beetles), the evidence that badgers transfer the disease to cattle is completely circumstantial and at the time of writing there is no final proof that such a transfer takes place.

None the less the discovery of this first dead badger indirectly put badgers under a much greater threat than before the passing of the Badgers Act. Although the Ministry of Agriculture stressed that the bovine tuberculosis problem was very localized, inaccurate publicity amongst farmers led to a general feeling that badgers were to be feared as 'carriers of disease'.

To me the whole affair was blown up out of all proportion, and has created a serious situation for the badgers of this country. Although it is illegal, some farmers took the law into their own hands and gassed all the badgers on their land 'just in case'. The persecution of badgers by digging has decreased considerably since the passing of the Act, but an increase in snaring on many estates (illegal, I maintain, under the cruelty clause of the Act) together with the tuberculosis scare means that badgers are still seriously threatened.

When I was asked to take Baloo from a 'clear' area of Wiltshire and to return her to the wild, I knew that it was unwise to move a badger from one part of the country to another, even from areas regarded as clear, unless the animal had undergone tests for tuberculosis and been declared free from *Mycobacterium bovis* by the Ministry of Agriculture.

Marion Browne, a Wiltshire naturalist, who had looked after Baloo from the age of ten weeks, approached me. She was anxious about the future of her badger as well as of the species as a whole. She was aware of the need for Ministry of Agriculture clearance, and took great trouble to have her badger tested, providing the officials with urine and faeces samples as required. Such tests, I fear, are inconclusive, for if a badger eats the dung beetles from an infected cowpat, it may retain the bacillus in its gut and pass it through the digestive system into its own dung pit, where its infection is out of harm's way. Only a post-mortem which reveals tuberculosis in the badger itself is conclusive. Rarely can the Ministry of Agriculture have had the opportunity of obtaining repeated samples of fresh badger urine, and their slowness in declaring Baloo clear may have been because they wished to improve their methods of detection. Great patience and skill are needed to obtain these urine samples and no doubt Marion's technique was well worth watching.

Eventually, as the weeks went by, and the chances of returning Baloo successfully to the wild were declining, I pressed Marion to obtain a final all-clear. This she did. To reduce the time it takes to transfer a badger of that age and to acclimatize her to a fresh person, we agreed that Marion should bring her up north and stay with her in my reception area. This, we hoped would provide the security a badger needs when moved to new territory. So it was Marion who introduced Baloo to her artificial sett and who was her sole contact for several nights. Baloo was provided with her own bedding in the sett, and a bucket of her dung was deposited near the entrance. Additionally, small 'toys', all exhibiting her own scent, vital for the acceptance of new ground, were given to her.

After several nights we considered that since I would have to take Baloo over from Marion after her three weeks' stay, it was time I made some contact. To preserve Baloo's natural caution, and to avoid instilling in her too much confidence in humans, Marion had been careful to make sure that she encountered no strangers. Now, I was to become her only companion. Somehow I had to break through the bond of confidence between Marion and herself. This proved no easy task, for Baloo, like all wild badgers, was extremely suspicious. However, although she never trusted me completely she transferred her affections sufficiently to allow me to complete her return to the wild.

At first Baloo behaved like a spoilt child. I would sit quite still in her compound, hoping that she would explore me. After the first initial fear, she sniffed me and I cautiously moved my hand (gloved, I might add!) towards her. She made a lightning snap at me and galloped back to her beloved Marion and musked her boots as though to say 'Who is that nasty person who is coming between us?' We repeated this routine several times, first exchanging gloves and other articles, until finally I put on most of Marion's clothes. But though Baloo was not to be fooled, gradually we made progress and slowly I was allowed to share in her relationship with Marion. Baloo treated me more as something to be tolerated if she was to have her nightly walks. As the nights passed, Marion faded more and more into the background and kept to a distance, while I came to the fore in Baloo's life. Finally, she accepted me, at times giving me the honour of her fun and affection.

Baloo loved her strolls through the woods and up to the fields, and after the first time quickly covered the route in her eagerness to get to the worms and the dor beetles under the cowpats. On wet nights, especially, it was fascinating to watch her pulling the earthworms from their holes with a quick jerk of the head. She would snuffle about until she found some, lying as they do on the wet grass with only their tails anchored, and then with a tug and a stretch she would jerk out the worms and suck them down like spaghetti. On one occasion, she devoured no less than 250 worms before midnight.

Having come from Wiltshire, where pasture and stubble fields formed her territory, Baloo was immediately at home when she reached the pasture fields beyond the oakwoods. In Wiltshire she had also encountered sheep in her nightly wanderings, so I was delighted to see that she completely ignored the sheep of the Lakes when snuffling among them for worms and dung beetles.

Unlike the worms which she rooted out with her nose, the dor beetles were eaten only after she had removed the cowpat with her feet, ploughing in it up to her 'armpits' and filling the evening air with the strong smell of dung.

It was interesting to note that she did not open all cowpats for she instinctively knew which of them contained the delicious beetles. I was sitting leaning against a rock watching her one teeming wet night when suddenly she realized I was there. Leaving her foraging she galloped up to me, with head and fore-legs covered in wet cow dung, thought it was time to play, and clambered up my back trying to remove my woolly cap. The smell from my cap and the back of my jacket now coated with dung was indescribable!

I gradually phase myself out of the badgers' lives enabling them to become completely independent of their foster parent. Generally I have only the electrical contact which, when they pass through the badger gate, rings a bell in the cottage to tell me of their presence and enable me to record their arrival. Occasionally I visit their setts by day to look for signs. On one occasion, as I approached, I heard the thudding of badger feet away from me down the tunnel. Maybe Baloo was lying near the exit and, being suddenly disturbed by voices, pounded away deeper into the sett.

The first sett which Bodger had dug in the woods was always adopted by her successors as their first natural sett after leaving the artificial one in the garden. At dusk I would sit out in the woods on a rock downwind of Baloo's sett, in the way that one watches for truly wild badgers. The night was still except for a slight current of air. It was almost dark, the robins were as usual the last to go to roost. I waited and watched and was soon lucky enough to see my companion of so many months emerge, wrinkle her muzzle at the woodland air, gaze at me with her bright black button eyes and nuzzle my bare hands for peanuts with her cold wet nose. Thus contented, she toddled away on stumpy legs up the woods along the tracks where I had guided her to the pasture fields and beyond, to feed on the worms and beetles which had become the largest part of her diet.

When my badgers no longer return I always feel very sad. I have given them so much care and attention and in exchange received tremendous pleasure. I know their ways so intimately and they have greeted me with such affection, yet their freedom is the very thing for which I have been working. Returning them to their own environment is so much harder to do than keeping them illegally as pets, dependent upon oneself. We are by nature selfish and would, deep down, feel honoured if they stayed and responded with affection. To put the badger first and be completely unselfish about returning it to the wild, parting with the creature to whom one has given one's all, both day and night for so long a period, takes strength of heart and courage.

It is quite an achievement to be able to spend each evening for approximately five months with a badger and send her away into the wild so discreetly that no one knows of her existence. The real reward comes when, after many months, one finds a sett which has lain empty for several years now reoccupied by a single badger. She knows you no more, but you know her. And when she is joined by a second badger the knowledge that the sett is again established and that a family of young Baloos or Puffles may once more roam the woods, the fields and the fells, is one of the greatest rewards of my work.

4

Signs of Spring

Whenever I walk alone in the country I observe many small signs of nocturnal life—the footprints, the part-eaten nuts and stripped fir-cones, for instance—that can lead me to the homes of many shy creatures.

On one walk, it was strange footprints resembling two dots and two dashes that led me from the lane through a hedge into a ploughed field where shoots of corn were thrusting through the surface. As I stood there in the morning sunshine I saw in the distance, moving beside the hedge towards me, a large hare bobbing along quite slowly, occasionally stopping to sit upright, ears erect, to check that no one was about. He was facing straight along the furrows and I quite expected to be seen by him. The hare's eyes are so much to the side of its head that it can actually see better behind than in front. This is a useful defence against unexpected attacks. Twisting this way and that, his long ears picked up warning sounds from across the fields. He came so close that I was able to watch his every movement including the way he placed his feet when bobbing along to make those strange padless footprints. My slight movement turned him from me, but he just ambled away across the ploughed earth and through the hedge into the adjacent land.

I was curious to see where he went and whether there were any others like him in the next field. Soon I was amply rewarded for my waiting, when what looked like mounds on the ground jumped up and started moving about. The hares were in a group in one part of the field, exactly as though a party of school children had gathered together in the playground for a game of tag or follow-my-leader. There were sixteen of them altogether and their fun-and-games were amazing. They would charge about, join up into one long string following the leader in an endless figure-of-eight, then break formation again. As if not knowing what to do next, one hare bobbed up to another which had started feeding, and invited him to a bout of boxing. So, standing up on their hind legs, they gave each other several lusty cuffs on the head. These antics continued for at least half an hour, and I wondered when they would ever stop to replenish the energy needed to carry on this display which plays such an important part in the mating ritual.

I continued on down the fields to a dell with a stream meandering at the bottom. This was the first time I had been here, and I wandered about underneath the trees on the banks, watching a robin and a wren flitting from the dead bracken to the decaying remains of fallen trees. Green spikes of bluebells were pushing through the earth and there were well-trodden tracks leading along the banks, passing under low branches and barbed wire with tufts of badger hair, to the pasture fields above. One could quite easily think that these tracks had been worn bare by the continual tread of a man's boots, but unless he were a dwarf that would have been quite impossible. Such paths may have given rise to the superstitious belief that little men and fairies live in the woodlands.

As I searched along these paths for footprints that would show the passing of some creature, I came across what looked like an almost perfect print of a baby's foot and I began to think that possibly there were little people in the dell after all. But, returning to my senses, I noticed that each print had five small holes about half an inch from the end of each toe, obviously made by the long claw of some powerful animal. The track passed under some elderberry bushes, and over a mound of bare earth to a hole in the bank. From inside came a weird sound of squeals and yelps, as of some young animals learning the art of tolerance in their confined existence underground. This was no time to disturb them, so I crept away intending to return at nightfall to see if I could discover what young things there were, living and growing in this small valley.

That evening as the sun was setting, I crept quietly through the fields and woods to the dell, trying to avoid the snapping of sticks underfoot. I decided not to go too near, and stopped with my back to a tree in a position where I could get a good view of several entrances along that section of the bank. All nocturnal creatures have a powerful sense of smell, so I was careful to get down wind of them with my back to the stream. The sun had set behind the trees and one by one the birds, with the exception of a singing robin, were going to roost. Then, flitting quietly from branch to branch in the still evening light, and singing one or two more short bursts of song, even the robin settled down to rest as darkness fell.

All was quiet for a moment and then, a short way behind me across the stream, I heard rustles in the fallen leaves and the occasional sharp crack of a twig. I had expected the first sounds to come from in front of me, from the hole in the bank where I had heard the young squeals earlier in the day. But no, there were the distinct sounds of somebody or something coming nearer along the bank just across the stream. I did not dare to turn round to see if I could discern anything in the darkness. So I just pressed myself tighter against the tree. There were no whispers, as I would have expected if it was a young couple strolling together, but certainly something was coming closer.

Suddenly, from what seemed to be just behind me, a blood-curdling human-sounding yell rent the silence of the woods. My hair stood up on the back of my neck and my blood ran cold as I heard myself saying in a whisper 'My goodness, he's murdered her'. I stood there motionless, wondering what was to come. There were two more yells just as before. I froze to my tree. Then, after several seconds of silence, the footsteps receded until all was quiet once more.

By the light of my torch I went to investigate, creeping as carefully and as quietly as I could, down to the valley bottom.

Up on the other side among the trees, all seemed perfectly still. When I reached the top part of the bank where the screams had come from I found a number of gaping dark entrance holes with massive excavated earth platforms in front. These resembled the ones I had been watching on the opposite bank. Since I could find no signs of humans anywhere, I concluded that the terrible sound had come from the occupants of these underground homes.

In fact these setts were made by a badger, that large secretive creature of the night. The badger's long coarse grey coat would be almost invisible in the dusk, but his familiar white face with black eye stripes and white ear tips would have shown well if I had been able to peep round the tree. Later I realized that this blood-curdling yell was a mysterious, rarely used cry of his. Little seems to be known about this sound; some say it is connected with mating, but I feel this unlikely, as, in my experience, badgers make little noise at this time. This was the first and only time, in all my years of badger watching, that I have heard this strange call.

I stumbled back down the bank in the darkness, crossed the stream, and stopped beside the tree I had previously selected as being suitable from which to watch my chosen sett. Picking my way as carefully as possible I tried not to trip against any tree stumps buried under the leaves and dead bracken. But after so great a disturbance already the chances were slight that I would see the young creatures whose squeals I had heard earlier down the hole under the elder tree.

I had noticed that the rough trunk of the tree, which grew from the edge of the platform in front of the entrance, was scored white up to a height of about three feet, by the cleaning of many long claws. The yell from the other bank would be familiar to them no doubt, but my movement, however quiet, would not have gone unnoticed and it was possible that my scent had crossed their entrance. But I was prepared to stand and wait awhile.

In contrast with the earlier scream, the silence, broken now only by the brook, was a delight, and I waited motionless yet watchful. Barely ten minutes elapsed before faint rustles came from the direction in which I was facing. It was almost too dark now to see the hole behind the platform of hard earth, but there were other holes to the sides and below. From the lower one, almost hidden among the new grass and bluebell shoots, a rabbit came out and, quite unconcerned, sat just outside its hole and proceeded to clean its face and whiskers. Then it held up one front paw and groomed underneath its leg and down its side. After several moments it shook itself and began to take note of the world around, appearing to wonder what would be the best thing to do next. It would feel little hunger because it would have already been out once or twice during daylight hours to eat a few shoots of grain in the field at the top of the bank. Now it was content to dally under cover of darkness. The number of its enemies was lessened, and man in particular was not likely to bother it at this hour.

Some minutes after the rabbit emerged two large grey forms, like shaggy old men, appeared one after the other from under the elder bushes, and ambled up a side track through the brushwood to the field above. In the beam of my red torch I glimpsed the two badger occupants of this sett. Without this light I would certainly have missed these wanderers of the night. Their tread was silent on the hard packed surface of the badger path, trodden for many years by their large flat feet, and as far as I could make out, they did not pause to scent the air, though I may have missed this in the darkness.

The night was getting chilly. My chances of seeing the young things I had come to watch had slipped by, so after the disturbances of the evening I left the woods, determined to visit these creatures another night. At least I knew that badgers lived in the sett, so possibly their young were there also, kept underground until much later in the night.

Heavy rain the following night dissuaded me from visiting the dell. Not only would I have become soaked within minutes, but the vegetation was dripping wet and the swollen stream in the foot of the valley would be too deep to cross without the water coming over the top of my boots. On damp nights there are advantages in watching wildlife, as a humid atmosphere makes one's tread over the leaves and bracken almost silent, but continuous rain makes conditions impossible for watching.

I did not wish to leave too long a pause between my visits, so I went along two nights later. The fresh scent of herbage washed by the previous rain made the evening pleasant and the earth smelt rich from its soaking. I was sure that the bluebell spears had put out more growth, and the grass between the patches of bracken hung heavy with the droplets of moisture. My footsteps made dark patches through the silvered grass as I walked.

Several blackbirds still sang, and between the clouds the sky was bright from the sun which had just dipped in the west. Down in the valley and under the trees it is always much darker than up in the fields, giving a false impression of the time of evening. But wild creatures always seem to take note of the general darkness, so that, except in midsummer, it is almost completely dark before they emerge.

I brought a cushion with me to sit on. A folding stool or chair is notoriously unstable for watching wildlife, as one of the legs almost always seems to sink into the ground, toppling one at the moment when absolute silence and stillness are essential. As so often in a dell where such creatures usually live, a slight breeze was eddying round the setts making it difficult to select a good position. If one is lucky enough to have a tree situated in a convenient place, its branches provide the most favourable position for watching badgers or any wildlife. From this elevated position any air movement will usually carry the watcher's scent over the top of the entrances, and one is less likely to be detected. Mammals like badgers or foxes seldom look upwards for their enemy, but keep their heads down as they move under the trees and shrubs.

I chose a position among the bracken next to a track leading down to the stream, looking towards all the setts. As I was situated lower down the bank I could not see the entrances, but only the tops and front of the earth platforms.

Approximately ten minutes after the last notes of the robin, a gentle stirring came from the sett directly in front of me. To my great surprise a small fox cub popped up from behind the platform and sat up on the edge, his large ears erect ready to pick up any sound of danger. Shortly after, a second cub appeared and stretched his long legs forward, holding his head upwards in a wide magnificent yawn, curling up the tip of his pink tongue, while his back legs stood upright with his long tail erect.

As I watched him straightening his cramped limbs, I yearned to do the same having sat for so long in one position not daring to move. Switching on my red torch to see more clearly, I discovered a third and fourth cub quickly joining the group and they all played for a short while at the entrance to the earth.

After a time the first cub, who was still sitting there, became bored and turned to do mock battle with one of the others who, completely taken by surprise by the sudden attack, turned his back on the attacker and flattened his ears in submissive posture. These fights, although playful, are nature's way of preparing for the time when, fully independent, they will have to defend themselves.

After further rough-and-tumble amongst all four cubs, first one and then another, tired and hungry, sat down to await the return of the vixen with some food. At some slight sound in the distance their ears pricked sharply as they craned forwards in the expectation of seeing their mother.

She made a wonderful sight carrying a rabbit to her young who crowded round eagerly. This was a scene we did not photograph then, for if she had heard, smelt or been the slightest bit suspicious that anything was wrong she would have collected up her cubs and transferred them to the alternative earth that all vixens have. Then my husband and I would have lost the chance of watching and photographing on subsequent nights.

As soon as she dropped the rabbit, two smaller cubs being the nearest, went forward to feed. They were immediately pounced on by a much larger and dominant cub who looked older than the other three, and who was determined to see them off and get her share before the others started. The noise was loud and long as a fierce fight took place, the yelps, squeals and little 'quacking' sounds breaking the night air. One cub was down on its back, with the dominant cub standing firmly over it, trying at the same time to drive away the second submissive cub on her left. Knowing that they were beaten, the two small cubs retreated back to the earth entrance limping and whining. After a while, one of the small cubs plucked up courage and again approached the rabbit but the boss cub swung her rear end round on to the little one and pushed it away. Peace returned as the dominant cub, whose presence indicated two vixens in the same earth, had her fill. The other three sat or lay curled up, awaiting their turn.

A slight sound attracted the attention of one of the cubs and almost immediately an adult fox appeared through some bushes a short distance away and, without pausing, descended on to the small track near where I sat. Quite motionless, I held my breath lest he pick up my scent as he came nearer. A fine russet

Bodger passing through her badger gate

Puffles plods off on his own; crossing a woodland stream

My two foxes playing together

Hedgehogs a fortnight old

brown colour with white front and underparts, he held his ears erect, though his head was low as he smelt his way along the track. Four feet from me the dog fox stopped dead in his tracks, sniffing the air in front and to the side, but as the slight breeze was blowing into my face, no scent of mine reached his sensitive nostrils, so he resumed his stroll along the path, making a slight evasive movement as though taking me for some new bush which had sprung up on his route during the day. After pausing to drink in the stream he disappeared from view. While this magnificent creature went by, I had kept absolutely still, but now I was able to relax with a deep breath.

When I returned the next night to the foxes' earth on the bank, two of the cubs came out and explored the bramble scrub which screened their entrance to the side. Pausing in their tracks they must have heard, I knew, the almost inaudible sounds of the vixen returning to the earth. She was a graceful animal slightly smaller and lighter than the dog fox. As she approached her cubs, they scampered up, flicking their tails and flattening their ears in an excited and submissive greeting, as though many hours had passed since they had lain curled up beside her. Taking little notice of their excited behaviour as they jumped around her, she looked severe and proud, giving an occasional sniff at their coats, before turning with a sharp bark and wandering back up the track. The young cubs remained obediently at the earth, having been told by their mother in this firm way to stay by the entrance and behave themselves. The vixen gave one more bark when she got to the top of the bank before disappearing into the field.

Then, out of its hole came the rabbit which, as before, proceeded to wash itself by the entrance. He took little notice of the fox cubs and they in turn ignored the rabbit. To have fox, badger and rabbit all occupying the same labyrinth of underground workings is not unusual. The fox often lives in the same passages as the badger, though their nurseries are separate. The fox is basically a lazy animal, who will share a badger's sett and occupy a section of the underground workings previously dug out or cleaned out by the badger. The badger is a clean and houseproud animal and will not tolerate a dirty sett, so it must be very irksome for him to have the decaying remains of the foxes' food around. A badger usually eats its food where it finds it and never takes it back to the sett. The rabbit is prey for both fox and badger but, since animals seldom hunt their food in the vicinity of their homes, they can all live amicably even in such close proximity.

For about three hours I watched the four little foxes at play, bowling each other over with puppy-like snarls, taking part in mock battles and in serious fights over their food, and sometimes just sitting and waiting for something to happen.

As I sat enthralled by their antics, I became aware of a slight breeze as the air cooled after nightfall. I hoped that this would not cause my scent to be blown towards the foxes. Suddenly from some distance away, in the field at the top of the bank on which the fox cubs played, a single staccato bark rang out and was repeated several times at intervals of a few seconds. The first call, the vixen's warning of danger, sent the cubs scurrying underground for cover. Out hunting in the fields she had picked up my scent and conveyed her fear of man to her cubs at the earth. Wild creatures seem to be extremely effective at instilling absolute obedience into their young, and without such teaching many a young animal would be killed by a predator. The vixen continued to pace backwards and forwards across the width of my scent over the field, giving out her intermittent call of alarm to her young, and so keeping them underground until she considered the danger had passed. At her persistent calls, I took the hint, and gathering up my cushion, I crept stealthily away, leaving the little family in the dell in peace.

One aspect of spring which amuses me is the most unexpected scale of the spring migration of toads from their places of hibernation to their breeding pool. With one accord they seem to choose my garden pond as the place in which to meet and perform their nuptial display. One rather cold night in March, I happened to go down to the pond with a torch, on my nightly sortie round the garden.

Suddenly I saw the head of a toad, its protruding luminous golden eyes shining in the beam of my torch. Scanning the water I found several more toads about the same size, some swimming and some resting, and one very large nobbly toad with her smaller, more dainty partner on her back. I watched and listened to a most delicate music coming from all over the pond, and was reminded of some operatic performance. The mating pair were the central performers, the male singing his solo to his loved one, his light chirping song interspersed with watery bubbling sounds as he breathed out, submerging his head for a few seconds. Fourteen other males were arranged all round the pond with eyes shining, resting on various clumps of weed and stones, every one emitting a different musical note, and providing the chorus and background for the soloists. Some were totally submerged, producing a soft chirring sound like that of a grasshopper warbler, while one or two frogs grunted the base notes, harmonising with the croaking melody of the trebles. The drums were represented by many more anxious toads banging against the surrounding wooden fencing which divided the garden and pool from the rough track beyond, in their eager endeavour to reach their spawning ground in my garden pool.

The total performance was most melodious to my ears but I could not leave all these toads and frogs to spawn freely if the eggs laid by the fish, the permanent occupants of the pond, were to develop unmolested by the voracious appetite of tadpoles. Although tadpoles of both species are vegetarians in early life, they soon become avid feeders, even to the extent of cannibalism. In spite of the removal of the performers from their concert platform, more and more toads arrived nightly. I found frog spawn at one end of the pool and toad spawn, in long clear glutinous strands studded evenly with black beads, was everywhere wound around the clumps of weed like tinsel around a Christmas tree.

Eventually I transported the toads in a bucket up into the woods to other pools where I hoped they would carry on their courtship. This concentration of toads provided such a sound of chirping and spluttering (the bucket contained fourteen mating pairs in all) that I made a recording of their delightful spring song.

The night was dry and still and, as I walked with my musical load through the oak woods, there came a sound as of raindrops pattering on the ground. Since I could feel nothing, I stopped and looked and listened. There was certainly much tapping

63

and rustling on the woodland floor and I was amazed to find that in place of raindrops, the sound was made by other toads responding to the music of my orchestra and choir. The wood must have been alive with them. I felt for all the world like Gulliver being surrounded by the little people, and I made my way among the toads to the shallow leaf-covered pool where a pair of newts had already made their home and frog spawn rested among the leaves. I placed a mating pair in the water, and distributed the remainder of the struggling, singing males around the area, facing away from the water. By the light of my torch I watched fascinated as they turned and marched in direct line until they rejoined the others in the water. Then I turned and left them to their music.

5

Young Foxes

The opportunity to study foxes in some detail arose unexpectedly as a result of a telephone call from my daughter-in-law, who then lived many miles away at Birmingham University. By her excited tone I knew she had some unusual news. Both she and my son, who developed a keen interest in insects as a very small boy, are fond of all forms of wildlife.

The telephone call turned out to be a request for help. Some fellow students, working with a farmer to dismantle a hayrick, had come across five small grey furry creatures with long tails and blue-grey eyes in the stack. At first they thought that the farm cat had left her litter inside the rick, but soon realized that these creatures were not kittens. It was suggested that they might be fox cubs. Closer examination revealed one female and four males, and as the farmer did not want them, they were taken back to the University to be fed and cared for until their future was decided.

When she saw them, my daughter-in-law immediately rang me up to ask me if I would like to rear one of these baby animals, and I replied that I would not like one, but two, as I feel young animals should always be reared in pairs, as this gives them the opportunity to play and develop with their own kind. So she took two of these creatures home, and as soon as I was free I motored down with a large wooden cage in the back of the car to collect some unknown animals which might possibly be foxes.

My daughter-in-law greeted me at the door and led me into the kitchen. The two rat-like specimens were lying on newspapers alongside a central-heating stove which served as a substitute for their foster mother. I identified them as fox cubs. Their teeth showed that they were about four weeks old, though they were very small for their age. We gave them a feed of milk, raw egg, and wholemeal bread, and shortly afterwards I departed with my cargo of fox cubs snugly asleep in their box of straw on the long journey back.

Arriving home in the early hours of the morning, I gave them another small feed and popped them into the hut in the garden, where I had provided a bale of straw to make a wall for their sleeping area, a tray of soil, and a bowl of fresh water. Then I went to bed, hoping to examine them more closely the following day.

Next morning I was up early, eager to see what I had brought home. Through the window I could see two charming bundles of fur staggering round the floor, exploring their surroundings. They looked up when they saw my face, but took little notice and resumed their exploration, making unsuccessful attempts to climb up the bale of straw.

Using Farlene (a useful standby for most young things at weaning time) raw egg, glucose and warm milk, I prepared a meal and took it in, wondering how they would receive it. They had already had contact with several human beings, so they came forward hungrily as I put the two dishes on the floor. Their short noses seemed to get into the mixture causing them to splutter and draw back, and their manners where not all that they could have been, but after all, they had not had much practice in eating from dishes. Undeterred, they made many more attempts, and soon learnt the right way to get the food into their mouths without it getting up their noses at the same time.

After they had licked their dishes clean, I picked up each cub in turn and examined it to check its condition. The little dog seemed well, and though he did not have much flesh under the skin, his eyes were bright and he was very lively. The vixen cub had slight signs of mange above her eyes. No doubt their lack of size and weight was due to the fact that in the week since leaving their mother they had not received the nourishment she would have provided.

With many wild creatures reared by man, a change of food, and especially incorrect feeding, often causes stomach upsets in the early days, and unless one can stay and watch them for a while it is difficult, if there is more than one animal, to detect which has the diarrhoea. As it happened, both these two foxes were upset, and so as long as this persisted loss of weight would continue. I sought advice from my vet and obtained the right medicine to clear up the stomach trouble, as well as something for the vixen's mange.

Fortunately my vet has reared many wild animals and birds, so when I ring up with queries in connection with foxes, badgers, hedgehogs or jackdaws, he can usually give me most helpful advice. As a contrast, many years ago, I had a vet whose only advice was to put any young animal straight where it came from—into the wild. My reply was that I intended to do just that, but only when the creature was fit and well, and capable of looking after itself.

In the beginning, my two baby foxes fed three times a day, with the main meal at dusk. This was as near to wild conditions as possible. Their morning feed was the Farlene mixture I have already mentioned, but for the first week or so the last meal was of raw meat, and in addition I gave each animal a halibut liver oil capsule. This is invaluable as it provides the vital daily vitamins without being too oily. Careful treatment soon cleared up the stomach disorder, and one or two dabs of lotion cleared the mange. Soon the two foxes developed a cared-for appearance.

I made an out-of-doors compound for them so that they could play, inside and out. As I cleaned out each morning they romped together on the grass, stalking a buttercup head and pouncing on it as though it was a mouse. Although they had no mother to teach them all the essential tricks of survival, it was surprising how quickly they learned to hunt for their food.

When the young foxes were about three months old, I could not leave them alone in the outside compound while I cleaned out, as they were no longer satisfied with the space provided, and wished to explore the rest of the garden. They could climb up the wire netting at tremendous speed and get over the top and be away in a flash if not carefully watched. As soon as they had finished their play outside, I popped them into a large cage until the cleaning was over. When the cage was once more opened for their return, they dived round the corner and back into the hut which they now regarded as their home.

On one occasion, the little dog fox decided that he was not going straight back into the hut, and I stood holding the cage door open as he sat looking up at me. To encourage him I talked quietly to him, but instead of going directly to the hut door he made one enormous six foot leap to the top of the fence. Just as he was going over the top I grabbed him by the tail and hauled him back. He became alarmed at this unexpected treatment and gave off a strong jet of fluid from his scent glands, which resemble those of the skunk. The fine droplets were sprayed onto my clothing and skin, and it was a long time before I got rid of that pungent smell. Once back in the hut he was completely unperturbed, but it taught me not to trust his wily ways, and from then on I had to try and guess what was in his mind, and forestall him before he acted.

Gradually I reduced the daytime meals until eventually only one feed was provided at dusk. Sleeping most of the day, the foxes occasionally awoke to have a rough-and-tumble with each other, snarling and growling like young puppies. Though they swished rather than wagged their tails, more in the manner of cats than dogs, they would lay back their ears when in mock battle. Cat-like too, they sat neatly, very upright, with their four feet placed close together, their tails wrapped tightly round. They slept curled up with their tails placed across their faces.

The gradual change of colour in their coats as they became mature was very interesting. Up to the age of about seven weeks they were quite grey all over, but at eight weeks the red hair could be seen growing through. At twelve weeks they had almost lost the grey, and not only had they taken on the fox's attractive red colouring, they also developed their white underparts and muzzle, black spats, and the dark line from eye to jaw at the side of the nose.

Now their eyes were golden, their ears had grown quite large and pointed, and their noses were no longer short and puppy-like. Their tails were still quite thin, but red in colour. One thing I noticed was a small spot of black hair at the base of each tail. This not only marked the position of a scent gland but was the beginning of the black colouring of the long tail hairs which spread gradually until the whole tail was dark and bushy.

At twelve weeks old they were completely nocturnal, waking at dusk when I fed them on the food they would find in the wild. Although a number of helpers offered a variety of foods for them (mostly in the form of chicken heads and offal) I had no intention of giving them a taste for poultry of any kind, and preferred to give them natural food. I gathered slugs and worms and once a dead mole with the teeth marks of a weasel on its neck. Dead sparrows came from the nearby farm in plenty. This was suitable as far as dead food went, but the young foxes had to learn to catch and kill small mammals for themselves.

Using a couple of Longworth cage traps set just before dusk in the adjoining hedgerow, I obtained a plentiful supply of small rodents like field voles, field mice and shrews. The shrews I always released immediately, as I know the foxes would not accept them on account of their peculiar flavour. Incidentally, cats will kill and carry a shrew, but I have never known them to eat one. The only mammal I have actually seen eating a shrew was a badger. I put small live mammals down in front of the fox cubs as the first food of the evening, while they were still hungry, to make sure that they did not play with them but made a quick kill. When first introduced to the voles in their hut, the foxes were afraid of these fast moving intruders and took refuge inside their sleeping quarters. The voles who had no experience of their future enemies, explored their surroundings unworried. At last the young foxes emerged and started to follow the voles around the hut until they had become really familiar with their scent. The little vixen was the first to make a strike and, having done so, decided that vole made a very tasty meal. She was much more intelligent than her brother and quickly learned how to catch and kill for herself. As neither was given any other food until they had learnt their lesson, this did not take very long.

The little dog fox sat there watching the vole or mouse running round him and under his tail, never making any attempt to strike, presumably thinking that he would shortly be provided with a supply of his usual food, and so did not need to waste his time 'mousing'. He watched the little vixen efficiently catching her meal and at last decided he had better make an attempt. Once he had stirred his lazy bones, he soon became as proficient as his sister.

From this stage on it was very interesting to watch their eating habits. As each fox caught its prey, or collected up its sparrows it took them and hid them in the straw, or in any corner it could find inside the hut. The little dog fox was like a vacuum cleaner, picking up his sparrows about eight at a time in his mouth and walking off, his jaws bristling with legs and wings and feathers, to hide them in a corner. Both foxes, while busy burying their prey, kept a watchful eye on their partner, making sure that they also knew where his or her food was hidden. Neither would eat straight away, but left its own hoard, and immediately started to unearth its rival's. This resulted in several small fights.

The vixen had a very clever way of extracting the quarry from her brother. While he was engrossed in his meal, standing over his catch, holding it down with his front feet, and eating it, she would creep up near to him as though to pass him by. But as she drew level, she would swing her rear end round against him, making him lift his head. At that moment, she would duck her head down between her front and back legs, grab the food from him and leap away with her prize into a corner. This movement was carried out so quickly that only by watching her on several occasions did I see what actually happened.

I have already mentioned my beagle hound and his affection for owls. He was born with a strange and friendly disposition towards many living things. This first came to light when he was a puppy. He could never understand why, when he tried to make friends with a cat, he was met with an arched back and hisses. All he wanted was something lively to romp with. If the cat tolerated his advances, he would approach with wagging tail, sniffing and pawing in an invitation to play.

His encounters with the fox cubs were much more successful. He was only too delighted to have fun with them in the garden when they were small, and they in return would swish their tails and fuss round him making small whining sounds, as though he was just a large edition of themselves. The beagle began to look out for his playmates every time he went into the garden, and I hoped the cubs would not develop too strong an attachment to the hound.

As the weeks went by, I realized that this friendship must end. When the little foxes returned to the wild they would have encounters with the hounds of the local hunt and it was wrong to develop a confidence in this relationship. Their very existence would later depend on fear of the hounds, yet the only fear they showed in captivity was towards strange human beings, especially men. At least this showed that they had some defences though I would have preferred them to be even more timid. On principle, I never made any fuss of them, handling them only when it was absolutely necessary, as I had no intention of making them into pets, despite their attraction and charm. My desire was to watch them grow up as naturally as possible, and to study their development, character and behaviour.

Now that they were active only at night, sleeping by day in their barrel, they became very noisy and boisterous inside their hut, just at a time when the world is quiet and most people are asleep. Had they been in the open or in the woodlands, their play would not have been so conspicuous, but being confined to a wooden shed they crashed about playing fast and furiously. At times they behaved like monkeys, chasing at speed round the walls before dropping to the floor with a bang once more.

There were two small windows in the hut which were kept open for fresh air, but I had covered them securely with wire netting. When the foxes became very vocal, once they had developed their barking, the noise became quite disturbing. On occasions, they would jump up the walls and hang on to the netting, barking loudly into the night through the opening.

Although I was kept awake, my fear was not for my loss of sleep but for the neighbours who were not aware of the foxes in my garden. This noise at night made me anxious to release them, but I knew it could be fatal if they went into the wild before they were able to look after themselves completely. When they were five months old, two fine healthy young foxes, full of life and energy, the time had come to carry out my plans for their release. This was to be amongst the hills and woods and streams around my cottage. It is a haven for wildlife, though even here there are those who are prepared to destroy the creatures of our countryside.

At 9.30 p.m. on 1 July I prepared to release them in the large garden adjoining the oak woods. It was a fine dry evening. The sun was just setting behind the distant hills. I put their barrel against the wall dividing the garden from the woods and beside it I placed their supper. Although I did not expect them to eat immediately in such strange surroundings, at least there was food for them if they returned during the night.

I was anxious that they should go off together and not become parted and lost, so I picked them both up and placed them on the dry-stone wall where they could scan the surrounding territory. Immediately they jumped down into the long grass and bracken under the oak trees. I had seen them for so long in the confines of the hut that they looked very small out in the open. I stood on a rock in the garden and watched them trotting through the grass, keeping a careful eye on each other and not venturing many yards away.

The rocky outcrop over the wall, covered with bracken and grass, was their first playground, and as they gained confidence they chased each other, crashing through the bracken and up onto the top of the rock as if playing king-of-the-castle. Dusk was falling rapidly and they seemed to be making a tremendous noise, not only in the long grass but as they mounted and ran along the top of the dry-stone wall, clattering the stones as they went. Occasionally one of the foxes would sit down on top of the wall and look around in search of its mate. I thought that this was an unnatural position for a fox which usually uses anything, even a furrow in a ploughed field, to provide cover for its movements.

My husband and I continued to watch from the cottage window and the cubs provided much entertainment as they returned to the garden, playing games up and down the steep grassy slope. Occasionally they ventured through the gate onto the rough track, but obviously very insecure, they soon returned to the garden and woods. We watched until it was too dark to see, and eventually went to bed wondering if they would still be around the following night, or if they would go off exploring further afield. Next morning I was pleased to see that they had taken their food, but of course had not returned to their barrel; so I was intrigued to know where they were spending the day.

The following evening I was out on the rock waiting to see not only if they returned, but from which direction. As darkness was falling and the world fell silent around me I was startled to see a pair of ears appear over the edge of the far side of the rock. Gradually the face of a young fox appeared and I could recognize the shorter face and broader head of the little vixen. She was slowly followed by her brother, equally silent and stealthy in his movements.

I had placed a dead rabbit cut in half on a rock for them to eat so that I could observe them as they approached. They did not see me and I made no attempt to speak to them. They arrived together at the rabbit, the little vixen seized hold of it, but was snapped at by her brother. Quite by chance the rabbit had not been cut quite through, so a snarling tug-of-war ensued, until the rabbit came apart and each slunk off into the brambles to eat its meal.

Often in the subsequent weeks I would be awakened at night by their calls as they wandered round the garden and woodland, now playing less with each other but concentrating more on the serious business of searching for food.

Their territory did not enlarge for some months and I was delighted to find that throughout the summer and autumn they spent their days curled up against the dry-stone wall under the heavy cover of brambles and bracken, not a hundred yards from the cottage. I continued to put out a rabbit or other suitable food each night to ensure that they had some natural food and also that hunger never forced them to resort to stealing. As time went by they started to hunt separately, knowing that they would get more to eat by not having to share their prey.

I hoped to get one or two photographs of them in the wild and set up my camera and flash in the cottage window where I could see them as they returned during the night for their rabbit. Often I would sit up most of the night as the hours of waiting between each visit became longer and longer. By now they were very timid, and I have found it easier to photograph wild foxes.

The slightest sound, such as the click of the camera inside the window, even on the occasion when the flash failed to go off, would send the dog fox scurrying up the garden and away over the rock. This was most frustrating and his approach was even more cautious when he returned two hours later.

By December they were both fully grown and mature. The dog had grown a thick tail and a most impressive ruff around his neck. Both were in perfect health, large and handsome. The wild neighbouring foxes were small and scraggy in comparison, and showed the effects of poor feeding.

In late January, when there was a light covering of snow on the ground and the hills were white and majestic, the vixen came into breeding condition. The leaves had long since fallen from the trees and the frost was coating the branches with glistening white crystals. On such a night, I would hear occasionally the bark of a roe deer.

On one night when even the deer were silent, I was awakened at about 2 a.m. by the sharp staccato bark of the vixen, repeated at intervals of several seconds for many minutes. I could follow her movement in the dark, as her solitary voice moved about the rough ground around the cottage. Soon she was joined by the more husky triple bark of a dog fox who had come from his hunting in answer to her call. Possibly he was a hill fox, living some distance away. At this time of year his ears would be attuned to the wild shriek of the vixen. Quietly I opened the rear window of the cottage to take in the full significance of their conversation.

The calls were now coming from the garden, so close to the cottage that I could hear the low growls, snarls and almost mewing sounds which the vixen can make on occasion. By now the night was full of the sound of these two mating foxes. They seemed to be using every note in their register. Gradually their voices died away. I was glad to have heard the mating sounds of my vixen. After all, she had reached this grand maturity through the care and attention she had received since the day I first set eyes on her.

Fortunately for my foxes, hunting had been postponed since

the start of that season by the largest outbreak of foot-and-mouth disease that this country has ever known. This provided them with more time in which to learn the art of self-defence. But by the following March the hounds were once more filling the hills and valleys with their cry.

My vixen had left her bramble cover by February and taken refuge in rocky ground in which to have her young. I knew where she was living and, as she and her mate were the only two foxes in the area, any local resident who saw them knew where they came from.

The hunting fixtures were not advertised because the hunt wanted as few visiting followers as possible to reduce the risk of spreading the disease. One late afternoon just after the middle of March, I heard the sound of foxhounds in the distance. This came as a surprise to me. Had I been expecting the hunt, I would have gone up to protect the vixen. I believed that the hunt was unwelcome on the land and I knew she was well provided with food, and never showed any interest in poultry or lambs.

She was heavy with cubs, being only a few days off giving birth, but the fact that she was on private land offered her no security. To bolt her, the hunt's terriers must have been put down her earth. The report of the hunt said that they had put up a fine vixen, that she made little attempt to run and was overtaken within a few yards of her earth. The dog fox, which which was possibly lying out in the bracken nearby, was given a fast run over several miles, and as he took refuge in territory dangerous to hounds, the hunt was called off and he escaped.

I was disturbed by the attitude of the hunt in killing a vixen so near to her time. This action was, to say the least, highly unsporting. I had hoped to study her behaviour and that of her young, for she would undoubtedly have brought them to the cottage at night for food. In this way my study of fox behaviour was crudely and unnecessarily terminated, and so my detailed account of foxes' habits in the wild came abruptly to a close.

The British Field Sports Society's booklet *Foxhunting* by D. W. E. Brock gives the Masters of Foxhounds Association rule that where a fox runs to ground, it must be destroyed before being given to the hounds. I would therefore suggest that bolting a fox which is then immediately overtaken by the hounds is not in the spirit of this rule. Yet it is a practice which frequently takes place.

I appreciate that the hunt plays a significant part in the control of the fox population. In the rugged hills of the sheep farming areas the hunt is the best means of keeping the fox population within bounds. But it is a fact that the fox only occasionally takes a strong and healthy lamb, and more usually takes dying or dead young. They also take the after-birth if this is available, and may also pick up bits of blood-stained wool from the ewe. As a result fox scats and stomach contents show particles of sheep's wool, but it is impossible when analysing them to prove whether the lamb was taken alive or dead.

According to Roger Burrows in his book *Wild Fox*, the English dog fox weighs an average of 6.6 kg and the vixen 5.3 kg, so I would have thought that a healthy ewe could defend her lamb against the hill fox. On the subject of diet he shares my view: any lambs that are taken are sickly, very weak or stillborn. I have found, as did Roger Burrows, that when talking to farmers the visual evidence of a fox killing a lamb or a sheep is almost non-existent. Eating is no proof of killing.

Brian Vesey-Fitzgerald in his book *Town Fox, Country Fox* found dogs to be a much larger menace to sheep and lambs than foxes. Dogs kill an enormous number of sheep each year, a figure running into several thousands, in addition to the thousands injured which subsequently have to be destroyed. Recent figures from the Ministry of Agriculture, Fisheries and Food indicate that in one year 4,280 sheep and lambs were killed and 3,618 were injured in England and Wales by dogs.

Apart from the number of dogs brought into the sheep producing areas of the country by visitors, who allow them to run loose on the hills, one of the worst killers can be the sheep dogs themselves. In one area of Wales I witnessed an unaccompanied sheep dog drive fourteen sheep into a lake. They attempted to swim across, but all drowned before reaching the other side. On another occasion a sheep dog chased and caught a ewe on a small road, killing it and dragging it a few yards under a bridge below the road. There, over a period of days, it gradually ate it, running for cover every time we approached the bridge.

Another point is that a fox's normal diet consists of a large number of small food items: it is not characteristic for them to kill anything the size of a lamb unless they are absolutely desperate. Food taken consists of small mammals, birds, insects, carrion, rabbits, worms, slugs, caterpillar larvae and large quantities of fruit. They are opportunists, trotting about over the fields at night to forage—we have watched them doing this —and provided they can get enough in this way they are not likely to trouble about anything else.

The alternative to hunting would be wire snares, traps, poison and gassing. Anyone who has seen a vixen with her limbs broken and bleeding, caught in a spring trap dragging her half severed legs and trap behind her in an attempt to get back to her den, would consider death by hounds preferable. But modifications to the rules of fox-hunting could be made with advantage, so that they would still control the fox population and allow the hounds to have their outing without undue cruelty. For instance, if the hunted fox goes to earth it should be left, especially if it goes to ground in a badger's sett. To do anything else is to run the risk of killing the innocent and beneficial badger by digging out and wrecking her home, or destroying it by unnecessary stopping. One or two hunts are now co-operating where badgers are concerned and others should take a lead from them. The odds are that the fox will be caught on another occasion and perhaps a follower or two could be stationed to prevent the fox returning to the shelter of the same badger sett. This is often done when foxes use a particularly difficult rock crevice as a refuge.

Masters of Hunts should observe the very fine example set by the late naturalist and authoress, Miss Frances Pitt, who was Master of the Wheatland Hunt from 1929 to 1952, and heed her words in her book *Hounds, Horses and Hunting*. She states "We do not disturb the occupants (of a badger's sett) but whenever hounds meet within reach, we stop the sett with sacks stuffed with straw. These are pulled out again in the evening and hung up in a nearby tree ready to use next time. Once they were forgotten and the badgers pulled them out, tore them open, extracted the straw and drew it underground for bedding."

Frances Pitt never advocated war against badgers and considered it no duty of a pack of foxhounds to slay badgers. Her motto was 'live and let live' and she would leave the badgers alone. If, as on occasions, people protested, she would retort that her pack consisted of foxhounds not dachshunds.

She insisted "that the cleanly habits of the badger are the rule of every member of the species and, as an earth cleaner and preventer of mange, the badger is valuable to fox-hunting; it is also valuable to our country as an interesting member of its indigenous fauna and should be left in peace."

6

'Deer Close'

In the early morning light the elfin roe deer browse silently on the low branches of holly and ash beside the cottage, the flowering grasses still silvered with dew. Twin fawns born the previous May, together with the buck and the doe, make up the family group. As they feed, the parents are ever watchful, lifting their heads, with long ears erect twisting to and fro to detect the slightest sign of danger. Chewing stops as they sniff the breeze, shaking their heads slightly to catch any passing scent. The young feed on unconcerned and, as all is well, they continue their search for choice herbs among the plentiful long grass and shrubs. Brambles and ivy grow along the drystone wall at the edge of the garden, providing excellent feeding ground for these nimble creatures of the woodland. Many deer families creep up round the cottage to feed at dawn and dusk. Often they linger on, lying up during the heat of the day in the long grass and bracken, concealed from the eye of man.

The cottage, named 'Deer Close' because of its close proximity to the deer, is large, with a fireplace of rough stone. The countryside around is rocky and mountainous, a hard living for the sheep farmer, and the cottage stands on the slopes overlooking lake and hill, facing into the strong westerly gales. Leading from the main road the track is steep and rough. Remoteness gives the mind peace for which to be thankful. Here the wildlife can be seen and heard, the clock has little meaning, and the hours of daylight dictate the movements of man.

Majestic red deer, in groups as large as eight, have been seen from the cottage, but red deer have become fewer and do not often show their massive forms now. The larger pine forests and mountains are more attractive haunts in which to roam and feed. At many times of the year the roe deer, not a herding animal like the red deer, gathers in several family parties: a buck and a doe with one fawn; a doe with twins, her mate having been killed by poachers up in the woods, and feeding separately, an older buck and a one-year-old orphaned buck fawn with a lame front leg. He was injured in the early days when he followed at foot with his mother and stumbled taking one of his first jumps over a drystone wall.

Normally the young remain with the parents until the next year's young are due to be born, when the doe wanders off in search of solitude. During the rut at the end of July, the roe deer, in rich red summer coat and small cream rump patches, only visit the territory round the cottage in their pairs, and then only one pair at a time. There is rough grass round the cottage and they can be spotted out in the open at first light.

One doe browses peacefully; only a few feet away the handsome buck lies resting, yet never taking his eyes off her in case she moves away. At what seems to be a given signal, the doe darts away, and her suitor is after her, sprinting over tussocks and walls, long neck extended and head held low keeping close behind in line with her scent. Watching from first one window then the next I can follow their circular route through woodland and roughland until just as suddenly, the doe stops and starts grazing, while the buck rests, exhausted, close beside her. This pursuit continues on and off for several days until their circle becomes so small that it covers only about ten feet on the rough ground by the garden wall, as they follow behind each other at a trotting pace in an anti-clockwise direction. In this small figure-of-eight ring, mating takes place and the flattened grass around a central object, such as a tree stump, becomes one of the 'fairy circles', as they used to be called.

The finest example of family behaviour during the rutting season that I have seen also took place within feet of the cottage wall. On this occasion there were two families browsing in the long grass, selecting the purple thistle-like flowers of the lesser-knapweed. There was a single doe with a fawn. Her mate, a fine creature in the prime of life with an excellent head of antlers, had been killed by a car down on the main road the week before. The other family consisted of a buck of about four years, a doe and two charming, still dappled fawns. As I watched the peaceful scene, action suddenly started to take place. First, the buck chased the single doe and her fawn up the rocky hillside. Then he went over to his two offspring, browsing together in the long grass under a big ash tree, and with head down he drove them away behind a large rock. He now turned his attention to his mate having removed all intruders from his private life. The two long-legged fawns crept out from behind the rock and stood there in the bracken peering round in their desire to join their mother but not daring to disobey the buck's orders. The buck, impelled by his natural urge to breed, would not leave the doe in peace. This was for him the season when his partner was more attractive than at any other time during the year.

They had evidently spent a long time chasing each other because the grass was flattened as though heavy rain and winds had beaten it down. The grass was also a playground for the fawns, who had occupied themselves for hours in mock battles, putting their heads down together, pushing and testing their strength and agility on their long spindly legs, in preparation for the time when they would have strong antlers and have to duel in defence of their territory. But now the flattened grass became the stage for the mating of their parents. With his neck extended and his head held low, the buck followed so closely behind his mate as she trotted round, that his nose just touched her rump. The doe knew that her time was come and she stood quietly letting him mount her several times. Then she wandered slowly away from the nuptial ring and lay down in the long grass to chew the cud. The buck, having fulfilled his purpose in life, sauntered over by a small rock and lay there scanning his domain, the proud owner of a doe and twin three-month old fawns.

By the end of the summer the trees round the cottage become scarlet and gold and stand in a bronze carpet of bracken, and the deer whose red coats now blend perfectly with the autumn colours are less conspicuous. Soon these coats are shed like the leaves on the trees. Then the deer, in their thick grey coats, are the first, and sometimes the only, sign of life moving across the landscape at dawn. Their large white rump patches give them away, and when they lift their heads to feed on the lower branches of trees, or to look out for danger, their handsome white throat patches can be seen as well.

By December they have shed their old antlers and soon the young growth can once more be seen thrusting up through the crown of the head, growing almost visibly, reaching full size in about twelve weeks. When the new antlers are fully grown and still covered in 'velvet' (the hairy skin required to supply the nourishment for growth) the deer are at their most handsome. As growth is complete the deer thrash their heads against the trees to remove the now dead and dried up skin from their antlers, and the rough 'pearls' (spiky surfaces) and 'coronet' (frilly base) tear off the bark from the trunks of young trees.

The cottage stands in the centre of roe deer territory, and each season sees the cycle of behaviour, from the rut, the shedding and growing of antlers, the marking of territory by the bucks on selected trees round their perimeter; to the break up of the family in May as the pregnant doe once more seeks seclusion in which to give birth to her fawns. At this time there seems little activity. The yearling bucks have left the territory, the fawns lie camouflaged under cover of bracken and shrubs and remain completely still while the doe feeds quietly elsewhere, returning to her young at intervals to suckle them. Tremendous excitement ensues when we first glimpse the little Bambis, so small, no larger than hares but with long spindly legs and beautifully mottled coats making them almost invisible as they rest in the dappled sunlight. Occasionally we are guided to the very young fawns by the loud, persistent yelps they utter when calling their mother back to feed them. The fawns grow rapidly but stay close to their mother for many months, and even when almost fully grown will make piteous mewing calls when parted by some obstructing stone wall or fence. When I first heard this faint call as I stood hidden behind a tree watching the deer in the oak woods, my eyes turned upwards to the sky in search of a buzzard, and I was amazed to find so small a sound coming from an animal with which I had previously associated only the loud staccato barking which roe deer use when alarmed.

Next in interest to the roe deer round the cottage are the birds, and of all these the buzzard is the king of the woodland.

When working in the garden I hear mewing over the tree tops as a pair of broad wings glides into view, their primaries spread and upturned. In clear blue sky, these birds soar on the thermals with majestic grace and ease, rising higher and higher quite effortlessly, their mewing calls becoming fainter and fainter as they disappear from view.

To the farmer they are invaluable workers, taking young rabbits, mice, voles, moles and other pests back to the eyrie to feed their young. The buzzard's mostly hunt their prey from a tree top perch, where they sit and wait and watch, scanning the ground for the slightest sign of movement. Moles must surface more often than is suspected because buzzards, using sit-and-watch tactics, catch so many of them by making a pounce as soon as the mole appears on the surface. Also they sit and watch the starlings probing the ground for leather-jackets and earthworms, and immediately one is brought to the surface, the buzzard is down, frightening off the starling and gulping down the worm. So large and dignified a bird does not exert any more effort in his hunting and flying than is absolutely necessary. Young rabbits are carried in the talons but small prey like mice, voles and frogs are carried in the beak, and fed to the young in the nest.

Even in these enlightened days there are still farmers and gamekeepers who do not appreciate the value of many of our predatory birds and mammals. It was in a valley beside an oak wood that I watched two soaring buzzards take rapid evasive action as their feathers were split by the shot from the guns of two men hidden in the woods below. All birds of prey, including the buzzard, have legal protection, but some folk do not care or wish to know this fact.

On a clear bright day two pairs of buzzards, each with one young, soared mewing over the cottage and fells as I stood beside the pool at the foot of the lawn, fascinated to watch their movement and control of flight through my binoculars. When they climbed further away I thought I would try and call them back, remembering that, while watching a buzzard hunting over some fields, I had succeeded in doing so once before. On that occasion the bird had moved towards me from field to hedge, hedge to tree, and tree to tree just in front of me, replying to the calls I made from my hiding place behind a stone wall. The six buzzards above the cottage were moving away in effortless flight until they were beyond the valley beside the house. I mewed in strong high-pitched tones, and the breeze carried my calls in their direction. Their spiral flight was broken when one bird, with a tilt of the wings and tail turned, broke away from the group to glide over the cottage, head turning this way and that in search of the source of the mewing. The buzzard replied several times, but unable to see whence the call came, eventually banked over to the left and soared back to the party high up on the thermal. Majestic indeed and not to be fooled!

The air around 'Deer Close' is full of the song of birds in spring and summer, and I am always breaking away from the job in hand, attracted by some unusual call or song, to search the trees or sky for the signs of the species producing that sound. Long-tailed tits, seen in their family parties flitting about the tree tops in search of insects, making their thin but rapid high-pitched calls, are one of the most attractive little birds found anywhere. Working their way over the leafy canopy of the woods like an invasion of insect eaters, they appear on the scene, move across the trees, and fade away, their 'see-see' call becoming inaudible in the distance. Unlike most tits they are black and white and pink, and their very long tails seem quite unmanageable at times, flopping up and down as they move. When flying in small undulations from tree to tree in their large parties, their tails are straight out behind and give the impression of a handful of black and white feathery darts being thrown into the branches.

Early one morning in spring I saw two of these beautiful little birds as they plucked small feathers from a tawny owl which had been killed on the road. As I watched, they flew off up the hillside into the blackthorn scrub about a hundred yards away. I knew that they lined their nests with thousands of small feathers, and I thought how interesting it would be if only I could find the nest. I searched in the direction in which the birds had flown and was delighted to discover a most beautifully-made domed, egg-shaped nest, about five feet above ground against the trunk of a blackthorn bush. How these little birds had worked! The entrance hole was near the top and the nest was woven of moss and cobwebs. The outside was decorated to blend with the surroundings, and covered with many small pieces of lichen, appeared to be a complete lichen ball. It must have taken at least two weeks to construct. Although I was too late to watch the building and shaping of the nest, I observed the birds lining the inside with the tiny mottled brown and gold feathers of the dead owl.

A low spreading yew tree fifteen feet away afforded me enough cover to sit and watch the parents feeding their young. After parting the blackthorn twigs slightly and temporarily tying them back, I erected my camera on a tripod and positioned it about five feet from the nest. I settled down in my hideout to watch and take a series of photographs of the growing birds being fed. Increasing activity at the nest towards the end of a fifteen-day incubation period told me the eggs had hatched. Once the young were large enough to come to the entrance hole, feeding time was quite exciting and the grubs on the oak trees round about provided ample food for the young. Both parents came to the nest with food and as the young grew larger they could not wait for the grubs to be thrust into their gullets, but reached right out of the nest hole with wide open gapes.

Two weeks after hatching, the nest was becoming very misshapen at the rear, and I was concerned lest the young burst prematurely from the warm interior. On the sixteenth day there was great activity, and the parents remained for short periods calling continuously from the trees, as though tired out with the endless shuttle-service with food, obviously thinking it time the young emerged and learnt to help themselves. By mid-afternoon on this warm sunny day, it seemed they could tolerate the congestion no longer, so the first fledgling burst from the hole and flew to the nearest tree where the cock bird was calling. In the next couple of hours eleven fully fledged, very smart long-tailed tits streaked off, chirping furiously, and settled in the trees all around the nest. No wonder the nest was under such strain. How twelve fully grown birds managed to change position at all in that tiny fragile nest amazed me, but even more surprising, as they left, was the fact that they were all complete with their long tails. I knew that the hen folds her tail over her back when incubating the eggs or brooding her young, but where eleven young, plus one adult, all put their tails in so confined a space was quite a mystery!

This flock of fresh young birds was joined almost immediately by another large twittering family of newly hatched long-tails making the trees a flitting mass of some twenty-four long-tailed, dart-like birds, and the sunny air resounded to their high-pitched calls for food, until they moved slowly away out of sight and earshot.

In another season I remember the day when the great spotted woodpecker, the most handsome of woodland birds, drummed his favourite dead branch of an ash tree beside the cottage, breaking off every now and then to give swift chase to the hen who was making her chucking call, until together they sought a suitable tree in which they excavated their nest-hole and reared their young.

The green woodpecker, brilliant in its mating plumage of green, yellow and red, is timid yet highly vocal with its ringing witch's laugh carrying far through the woods as it guards its territory. Its keenness for ants makes it attractive to the gardener, and anthills are numerous in the rocky ground around the cottage.

At times there is a sudden commotion among the trees as jays, jackdaws, and starlings give warning of danger to the smaller birds. Then all rise in raucous terror, flying away as one from the onslaught of the sparrow hawk or, more rarely, the peregrine, both deadly predators of the birds of woodland and fellside. These hunting birds are no less attractive because they take other birds, although some people object to them for this reason. Their choice of prey—sparrows, starlings and many other plentiful species—plays an important role in maintaining the balance of nature.

On many a still spring evening after sunset, the grunting, followed by a sibilant 'tsiwick' of the woodcock can be heard. I watch him flying round the cottage over the trees and fells with a somewhat owl-like flight and curious interrupted wing beat in his 'roding' display. His nest is usually on the hillside among the silver birches, well hidden under bracken in a scrape on the ground. The camouflage is so exceptional that to go in search would be useless, and only by unexpectedly flushing out the bird while walking have I been able to find a nest. If the hen sits tight, it is unlikely she will ever be found, as she blends so completely with her bracken surroundings.

At dusk, too, from within the crook of a branch in a nearby oak tree, the tawny owl stirs and once more his hooting heralds the night. He must have been there all day, his mottled plumage hiding him from sight, tucked against the trunk of the tree. He repeats his long call a few times, the final phrase with a tremor in his voice, and as I wait and watch him, I hear his mate calling with her clear 'ke-wick' from the trees down by the lake. Except for his head which swivels round nearly full circle, first clock-wise then anti-clockwise, giving a wary glance in my direction every now and then, his large oval silhouette is motionless. In between his loud hoots he makes quiet muffled sounds to himself, or perhaps to me. Unseen and unheard in flight his mate calls, coming now from a nearby tree. She gives a series of loud 'ke-wick' calls, the last syllable on a higher note. No doubt the 'ke-wick' and the hoot from different birds in the same part of the woodland give the false impression that one bird is calling so leading to the mistaken idea that one owl produces the 'toowhit-toowhoo' call. In nature the 'ke-wick' and the hoot are seldom uttered close together, and always by two different birds.

When dusk has fallen the owl will shake itself and fluff up its feathers after its long daytime rest. Having stretched first one side and then the other, with wings outspread, it silently drops from the bough and with slow broad beats, steals noiselessly away up the woods in search of woodmice and voles.

One interesting predator of the woods, occasionally seen during the early spring is the white stoat, not yet changed from its winter coat. South of the Border it is most unusual to see these attractive and lively mammals in their coats of ermine.

From a nearby cottage window, my neighbour Mary, attracted by a white movement in the dead grass and leaves on the woodland floor, called me round to see the unusual sight. We saw the long white sinuous body with raised head cross the bank and disappear down a rabbit hole. The stoat's only marking was the black tip to his tail and a patch of darkening fur on the shoulders, as though he was about to lose the winter whiteness. Within moments he reappeared at the entrance with a small grey rabbit held by the scruff of its neck, dangling from his jaws. The stoat paused and jerkily looked around before darting off up the bank and out of sight. To enable him to carry the heavy load he had to run along in the shape of a letter 'S' with his long neck extended upwards. On several occasions I have seen a weasel crossing a road in front of the car, in this almost upright position, carrying a vole or a mouse to its young.

Within ten minutes the white stoat was back to the same rabbit hole, but his first appearance with the young rabbit had not gone undetected. From far above, a large brown buzzard had noticed the movement of the stoat and come down to a nearby tree to investigate. It sat on a branch and waited. The sharp eyes of the stoat did not miss this and he darted back into the hole. He dared not appear again with another rabbit while being watched, for he knew that the buzzard was after his prey and he was not prepared to part with that in a hurry. Several times the stoat came to the entrance of the rabbit hole, and with sharp bright eyes, peered about quizzically to see if the buzzard had gone, so that he could bring out his second kill and depart with it once more up the bank. Presently the large bird lost interest and with heavy wing beat, made off up the woods and out over the tops of the oak trees in search of other prey. Within seconds, the lithe white creature was out, carrying another young rabbit, and went with his load as before. He repeated this three times and, on investigation, I found his hole nearby among the rocks and the roots of a fallen tree.

Stoats normally have their single litter in late spring, so the fact that the winter had been exceptionally mild and food plentiful may, as with other fauna, have advanced the breeding season, although the stoat, like the badger, has delayed implantation, and mating may have taken place many months earlier. I believe that in this case, the young would not by then have been weaned and that the male was probably taking food for his mate who was no doubt suckling her young litter.

The *Mustelidae* family, which includes the stoat, weasel, pine marten, pole cat, otter and even the much larger badger, are extremely interesting members of our British fauna. On one occasion I was fascinated to watch a mother weasel crossing a busy road with her five young in procession, like a string of sausages on an invisible thread. They crossed the footpath in front of me, followed the kerb down onto the road, across and up the other kerb and into the hedge. Fortunately no cars appeared to break up the family convoy.

The weather forecast was set fine early one summer morning, so I rose at dawn to see the rising sun bathing the mountain peaks in scarlet, reaching down into the dark and sleepy valleys and flowing out into the lake below like molten gold. I wandered up the woods with my beagle at heel in search of any wildlife that there might be about at that hour. The occasional red squirrel could be seen feeding on the ground, but the slightest movement sent him scampering up a suitable tree to keep a watchful eye from the safety of its branches. Noting a woodpecker's hole approximately thirty feet up a tree I sat down to see if there was any activity. After several minutes I took my eyes off the hole for a second to rest my aching neck, when suddenly on the branch just below the hole was a chittering squirrel, twitching his tail from side to side and uttering his scolding noise. I never saw the woodpecker at the hole though the chippings of wood at the base of the tree were recently hewn, so possibly the little red squirrel may have popped out from inside. Once he had recovered from his initial shock, he showed little concern for my presence as he settled down on the branch in a reclining position, one back leg and one front leg hanging nonchalantly down. His tail lay along the branch in my direction, his eyes occasionally closed in rest, but also giving a casual glance in case I moved. Later, this red squirrel took to visiting the bird table at the cottage.

Leaving him to enjoy the warm morning sunshine, I strolled on up the woods. The occasional Scots pine and yew tree contrasted their rich dark colouring with the delicate light green and golds of the young leaves which now cloaked the trees in early summer. As I scrambled up the rough hillside, head down for a few moments as I climbed the bank, I was startled by the staccato bark of a roe buck crossing the slope some twenty paces ahead of me. Stopping dead in my tracks I watched him sniffing the air, trying to identify what clumsy object was attempting to pick its way up the slope over which he could leap so surely. Satisfied with his inspection, he passed on and away out of sight. I wished I had the effortless movement of an animal so perfectly suited to its environment.

I went on up the hill, my mind still on the graceful creature I had just seen. The dog was by now a few paces ahead of me, with nose to the ground as though hoping to pick up the scent of the deer. A few yards on the dog jumped back, as a big brown mottled bird flew up from the leafy ground and away up the slope to a large tree. I saw it was a tawny owl which on the ground was completely camouflaged in the leaves. On the wing it looked enormous and very conspicuous in the warm sunlight, a most unusual light in which to see a bird of the night. The beagle soon found where the owl had been and under a small overhanging rock on the ground were two snowy white owlets on their bed of dry oak leaves. The smaller crouched down into the leaves, like the proverbial ostrich, a white fluffy ball of down as conspicuous as it could possibly be. The larger of the two sat leaning against the side of the rock, eyes shut, making a continuous sharp clicking noise with its tongue. I went up closer and examined each one in turn. They tried to nip my fingers in self-defence, and after inspection I gently placed them back inside the sheltered hollow under the rock. The parent owl was sitting on a high branch of a tree nearby, being mobbed by jays and small birds. It was as well she sat there, her mind partly occupied by her tormentors, as owls are known to be quite fierce when their nest and young are being visited, and occasionally people have had their eyes clawed.

An attack from a bird with beak and talons as sharp as razors can inflict a very severe wound, as I had experienced many years earlier when walking down a country lane late at night. On that occasion I was nervous because rumour had it that this particular stretch of road was a sleeping-out place for tramps. I was running down the centre of the road in pitch darkness. The only sound was my footfall and hurried breathing. There were no cars on the road, so I felt moderately safe in the centre, though I was having difficulty finding my direction as I had no torch and there was no light from the sky.

Suddenly I felt a dull thud on the side of my head and some-thing soft enveloping my face. I can only describe the feeling, which is as clear today as it was the night it happened, as of a big cabbage with large floppy leaves entirely covering my head. This was followed by a sharp stab in the back of my neck. I screamed, but there was no-one there to hear my cries. I raced on downhill, clutching the back of my neck, my heart pounding. The lane seemed never to end. The light in the doorway of the house where I was staying was the most welcome sight. The wound proved superficial, but I was luckier than some, for only a week later another person was attacked and had to have stitches in his neck. The owl was subsequently found and shot as one dangerous without provocation. For years after this attack I was afraid of the sight and sound of owls, but now I am as enthralled with them as I am with all birds of prey.

The tawny owl in the woods by my cottage remained in the tree, and as I was keen to see her return to her young, and if possible obtain a photograph of her alighting by her nest, I hid myself under a yew tree only a few feet away. I waited for an hour with camera at the ready; but she had eyes as keen as a hawk, and just sat on her tree nearby staring back at me! I had thought I was well camouflaged behind the tree branches but she was obviously not to be deceived. A second person would have been useful on this occasion, because with most large birds if two people enter a hide and then one emerges and departs, the bird assumes that all is well and that the danger has passed.

Quite recently I had yet another interesting experience with a tawny owl. One evening after dark I could not find the dog anywhere, so I put on the outside lights round the cottage and went into the garden to call him. There had been heavy rain for the past two days and the nearby stream, tumbling down in full spate, drowned my calls. So I used my 'silent' whistle, which emits a high-pitched rather weak note, audible to the ears of a dog some distance away. I stood on the large outcrop of rock, in the light of the lamp which hangs by the door. No dog appeared but, instead, a large mass came flying round my head, and remained about eight feet away in circling flight. It stayed with me while I continued to blow my whistle and when

I stopped, it flew off into the oak trees behind where I stood. This large brown owl must have mistaken my high-pitched whistle for the supersonic squeals of a vole, which he was hunting as the main part of his evening meal. After several minutes, the dog returned from the darkness of the night and into the glow of the cottage.

Down in the valley below the front window of 'Deer Close' the lake lies stretched out, reflecting on its surface the moods of the elements. It tends to set the tone of one's feelings. Sometimes it is grim and colourless with threatening storm clouds and grey mountains, and sometimes it becomes a mass of moving water, the surface covered with leaping white horses as the wind lashes up its length from south to north. In the evening after a rough day, the low sun from behind the heavy clouds sinks beyond the darkened heights to the west, covering the lake in a warm orange glow, touching the surface of our hillside with its gold, and bringing the rocks, trees and bracken into strong relief in the slanting light.

At other times, thunder rolls round the mountains like a mighty giant with a sledge hammer, sending sparks of fork lightning. Brilliant blue and pink sheets of light, illuminating the lake below, silhouette the mountain ranges against its brilliance. Then, the clouds are ripped apart drenching the earth with rain, turning the streams and rivers into raging torrents which tumble down the rocky mountain sides into the lake, raising its surface and drowning its edges and islets.

A mood of tranquillity comes in the morning when the water can become as still and clear as a mirror, reflecting soft subtle colours, and a ribbon of cloud rests between hilltop and water, waiting for the sun to rise and melt it with its rays.

On one such occasion in late winter, we awakened to a brilliant sunny morning. A plume of white mist lay on the lake below the cottage and the pine trees on the far side pricked this soft blanket with dark spines. Wetherlam and Langdale Pikes were pure white above the mist after a heavy fall of snow during the night. But now the larch trees below the window are growing fast and sad will be the time when, if unchecked, they hide the lake. At present we watch the wild duck in great numbers: mallard, tufted duck, pochard and merganser, coming and

going in their seasons. The greylag geese pass to and fro from
tarn and marshland to estuary, calling to each other as they
go, and the majestic swans fly up and down the lake as white
arrows skimming the dark surface of the water.

The shore on the far side has many promontories and small
islets where the grey heron stands like a statue, waiting for small
fish to pass within its reach. There, too, the stately cormorant
is poised with half-opened wings drying in the gentle breeze
which eddies round the forelands. By the early light in the
field across the lake, the red deer feed in a herd of seven or
eight, always moving nimbly back over the wall into the trees
before the farmer arrives to tend his sheep which rightly own
the pasture.

Pheasants live and breed in the woods across the lake and
their excited call carries over the water. Many is the time we
have watched as these colourful birds rocket upwards out of
the trees to make their dash for cover across the open field to
the woods behind the guns. As they fly low over the treetops,
there is a series of white puffs followed almost immediately by
several sharp reports. Occasionally we see the birds reach the
cover of the woods, but usually they come plummetting down.
Each colourful ball of feathers is left to flounder on the grass until
the men are sure there are no more birds to come, and then
with a word from his master, the faithful dog trots off to retrieve
the prize and return with it to his master's feet. The pheasant
is game indeed for the table, and lives a life of freedom in the
copse or cornfield until the moment the shot crumples his limbs
in death. The tragedy is that, even today, the pheasant is the
only bird which must be cared for, in the minds of some of the
keepers who rear and guard these birds. Native creatures with
hooked beak and canine teeth are still destroyed in the cause
of the alien pheasant. Much depends on whether the keeper's
training has been handed down from father to son, or whether
the landowner and master cares not how his servant achieves
his results, or whether the keeper has been trained to have a
more enlightened and humane approach to predator control.
The gin trap and pole trap, though illegal, are still used, while
snare, poison and gassing are the simplest, most common and
most indiscriminate ways of disposing of all living things which

occupy an earth, sett, or hole anywhere within a wide area around the pheasant breeding pens or copses.

I have witnessed the ghastly sight of a suckling sow badger dead in a lock snare, leaving a litter of cubs to die of starvation. The farmer who showed it to me considered that it had taken several days to die. The hide of a badger is extremely tough and to have cut through the skin and the thick layer of fat below, as the badger struggled to release itself, the wire must have caused a slow agonizing death. Another badger on a different estate was completely disembowelled when the running-snare tightened relentlessly around its stomach and cut through to the spine.

Both the lock and running snare are extremely cruel, and when used for badgers, in my opinion, should be considered illegal under the Cruelty Clause of the 1973 Badgers Act. However there is another and different type of snare which can be used humanely for catching mammals. This is the stopped-snare which has a soldered stop positioned to suit each type of mammal. The loop will only close down to the size dictated by the stop and so will not damage the animal but merely hold it. For instance, when set to catch a fox, a ten inch length of wire is needed up to the stop and this size loop will hold a fox, which is neither damaged nor excited, until the keeper arrives in the morning to shoot it. All snares set at night should of course be inspected early in the morning when the animal is either released or killed. Many enlightened gamekeepers and estate officers are now rejecting the lock-snare and the running-snare and are using only the stopped-snare which is both human and effective.

Using nineteen inch stopped-snares over three nights, a family group of eight badgers were caught successfully and transferred from a place where they were endangered to a safe and suitable reception area. So gentle was the method that all the badgers were quite placid in the snares when collected early the following morning. After being kept for a few days in a loose box, all the badgers were released into an empty sett fifty miles away, not near other badgers and the colony flourished in its new home. Without this move they would have perished.

Gradually the younger gamekeepers are becoming more tolerant and appreciative of the place of predators in the natural order of things. The older school of keepers is astonishingly cruel, using barbarous methods, neither seeing nor caring about the agony they cause, but merely adding the carcass to their list. British mammals like badgers, stoats, weasels, foxes and hedgehogs should not be controlled in the interests of breeding the alien pheasant for game. Little does the keeper realize that for every badger, owl or hawk he destroys, he spares the lives of rodents which suck his eggs and kill his chicks. He slays the very friend of his flock.

At 'Deer Close' the month of October brings us the bellowing call of the red deer stag in the rut, carrying over the water and resounding round the hills and fells. The sound is of the wild and of wild places. In winter time, the cottage stands in the teeth of the gales which sweep across the lake from the south west. The bare trees in the woods at the side sway and groan, and those with shallow roots cause the whole earth around to heave with the movement of the tree above. One or two succumb to the gales and fall with a crash, sometimes stripping the branches of neighbouring trees; on others, single branches of oak and ash can hold on no longer, and split away from the tree, leaving a nasty gash in the trunk. Clearing the woodland floor after the storm is always an enjoyable though hard task, and nothing usable is wasted. The sawing, splitting and stacking of logs for the fire is strenuous work, but the sight of the evenly stacked logs drying against the cottage wall is reward indeed. The large oak pieces when seasoned are sawn up for making furniture in the home.

'Deer Close' stands on the mountainside surrounded by the wildlife which chooses to seek its shelter and friendship, and from here many creatures have been returned to their natural environment.

7

Blackbird Predators:
Town and Country Style

One afternoon in April I was discussing some problems with a naturalist friend on the telephone, when from the garden came a tremendous clucking in the hedge beside the summerhouse. Putting down the receiver I dived out into the garden, to find great distress among the parents and seven-day-old chicks of my blackbird family. Last season my handsome pair had repeated bad luck. They built four nests, each with $2\frac{1}{2}$ to 3 lbs. of material, but the hen laid eighteen eggs before successfully rearing three young to fly. On every occasion, as soon as the eggs were laid, either a magpie robbed the nest of its eggs, or a sparrow punctured them with a single hole. Only after building her fifth nest did the blackbird finally rear her three young. All was going well this year.

But now a magpie had scrabbled right inside the thorn hedge and within seconds had picked out three chicks and decapitated them, leaving two strewn in the watery hedge bottom and carrying one twenty yards from the nest. The hedge was quite literally dripping with blood so they must have been beheaded in the nest. A fourth chick when first seen, was hanging upside down with one foot caught in the nesting material, but finally landed among the tussocky grass at the base, where I found it huddled motionless in water under a half-submerged clump of grass.

As the parents were clucking round in fear and panic, I put this little one, which at first seemed to be uninjured, back into the nest and returned to the shelter of the summerhouse to watch if the parents would return to feed it. The hen by now had fled, leaving the cock 'pinking' round. Eventually he settled down to collect caterpillars, so at least there was some hope. Very cautiously he worked his way up to the nest with his small offering, but when he saw no signs of life, let alone a gape eagerly waiting to receive these grubs, he flew off and consumed them himself.

For well over an hour I waited and watched, but there was neither sound nor sign of either parent nor movement in the nest. I had to make a decision there and then. Was I to check whether this little chick was still alive and if so, take it and hand rear it and return it to the wild, or leave it to die of cold, hunger and fright alone in the nest? The latter was quite unthinkable to me, so I put my hand into the nest and removed the still warm but motionless little bird.

Using a small cardboard box with a rough towel laid over a hot water bottle in the base, and an old woollen sock curled round, I prepared a nest in which I carefully placed my fledgling. By evening he was stirring and, when I opened the box, his head was waving round and he was making small pathetic cheeps in contrast to the loud noises he had made when hanging from the nest in the hedge. Several small worms which I offered evoked no response, and his beak remained sealed. Then I found that by squeaking myself, he opened wide his gape and I could thrust the worms down the little throat using blunt tweezers. He ate three more small cut-up worms, and feeling better already, stood up and up-ended his tail, while I waited patiently like the parent bird until he passed a small white parcel wrapped in a gelatinous sac.

His last feed of worms that night was just before midnight and I was up again by five wondering whether he had survived. He was alive but weak, and only ate a very small amount of egg yolk mashed up with digestive biscuit crumbs. When I returned at 8 a.m. he was showing signs of recovery and ate some more cut-up worms quite lustily, and was by now cheeping again. As the hot water bottle was inside the box, it meant disturbing him every time it needed refilling, so I resorted to a square biscuit tin with electric light bulb and thermostat inside on which I placed his box. This kept the temperature constant and served my purpose well. He went from strength to strength, becoming vociferous, demanding more and more food. He was weakest at his dawn feed as he seemed to find the night very long, although he would not have been fed after dark by his parents. On one or two occasions he seemed too weak to stand, but by eight o'clock he had recovered sufficiently to be voicing his requests and hopping about inside his temporary home.

Next, I transferred him from his box to a wooden breeding cage and reduced the heat. I was thus able to keep an eye on him without having to open the lid every time which, to him, meant food. As the garden was very dry and his demand for worms increased, I went to the fishing shop and bought a jam jar of maggots. A friend gave me an open invitation to visit her manure-cum-compost heap whenever I wished, as there was a superabundance of worms, far beyond the needs of my all-important little fellow. He ruled my life for the next three weeks or so, with his demanding appetite, so much so that when I had to attend meetings, I took the cage with me in the car and every now and again bid the chairman excuse me for five minutes or so while I went to feed my bird!

By now he was fed every hour from dawn till dusk, and as soon as I went near his cage he would sit on his perch, flicker his wings and open his beak. Opening the cage door I poked into his gullet the worms or maggots as quickly as I could, until his crop swelled visibly and the worms could be seen squirming about inside as it altered shape and the feathers rose and fell. When satisfied, he shuffled sideways in crablike fashion to the far end of his perch, head turned away like a peevish child who wants no more rice pudding! His eyes closed gradually and his legs sagged until he sank into a doze, while his crop took over the next part of the digestion of the worms; but it seemed only three or four minutes before he was up and chirping again for more.

Whole maggots were not digested, and passed straight through his system, but I found that by giving them a slight tweak, breaking the outer skin, he was able to absorb the nourishment within. At this stage he also enjoyed soaked currants.

The magpie ordeal had not left him unscathed, and he had a slightly twisted beak, which stayed open and did not meet at the tip, as a constant reminder. He could cope while hand-fed, but I was concerned for his future when he would have to pick up his own grubs in the wild. Although his plumage grew well and he was developing a luxuriant covering of feathers, his right wing never grew any secondary feathers, thus leaving a large gap between the primary and tertiaries. Scaly quills still covered his wing feathers, and between feeds he spent his time in preening, running his beak down the length of each feather to the tip to loosen the covering, leaving what appeared to be a pile of grey scurf on the cage floor.

After about a fortnight his tail feathers began to grow, so I knew that in normal circumstances he would have been ready to leave the nest. I wondered how I could wean him from having worms poked into his gape with his head held upwards, and make him look downwards to the cage floor and take notice of food placed there.

So one morning I wedged a piece of soft wholemeal bread between the bars of his cage to see whether he would notice it. After about five minutes he took one or two pecks in a rather desultory manner and finally left it. The next thing I noticed was my dog circling round the cage, in which previously he had taken little interest, while the blackbird watched with a bright eye. When the beagle thought neither I nor the bird was looking, he gently pulled the bread from between the bars and ate it quickly. From then on he kept a careful check on the bird's diet to see that it was not receiving food which rightfully belonged to a dog.

When I dropped a worm, which wriggled and writhed about on the floor of the cage in front of my blackbird he noticed and made several tries to pick it up, but his aim was bad and his beak would not meet round the worm. Putting down larger and larger worms I found that he could pick some up, and after thrashing first one way and then the other he managed to break off pieces and swallow them.

Now I tried him with maggots, putting them in a dish with a little water to wash off the bran in which they were kept. The maggots moved so quickly that I had to give each one a slight squeeze to prevent them from climbing out, but this did not stop them from moving entirely and the bird saw them. He became quite keen, and after flicking each one in turn, sometimes sending them all over the cage, he eventually got the knack of picking them up and eating them quickly.

The dish with the maggots was about as long and as wide as the blackbird, and after a time, whenever a fresh dish was placed in the cage, he would leap down off his perch and trample around among them, then shuffle down and start bathing, throwing the maggots all over the place. I realized that he wanted a bath, and placed a second dish in his cage. Within seconds he was flicking water around, taking on the appearance of a drowned rat. This showed up the thin and missing plumage, and although he shook himself afterwards he certainly looked as though he had just been fished out of a river, and made no attempt to preen himself. Observing how poor his plumage was for a bird which should now be flying, I started giving him cod liver oil, which I administered by first wiping each worm in oil before his feed. After a week he took on a more cared-for appearance; he became glossy and groomed, though he never grew all his missing feathers.

I now gave him the freedom of the garage in which to exercise his wings. There were several shelves high up on the walls with branches fixed to them. He had made no previous attempt to take up his nightly roost above ground level, so I would go in at dusk to make sure his crop was full and to help him up onto the highest perch for the night. I put his worms out on a thick rubber mat on the floor to simulate the softer ground on which he would pick up food in the wild. As soon as I went into the garage he flew across and onto my shoulder or head, chirping expectantly, while I tipped out worms and soil onto the mat, for him to scratch among. He became very excited, jumping about, and cocking his head from side to side as he looked up at me and then down to the floor. Occasionally he would give a short sharp jump onto the soil and quickly back again, to stir it up so that he could see any worms or grubs, or pick up a lump of soil or leaf and flick it far and wide, to see what was underneath.

He had now no problem digesting maggots and he picked them up from the floor as fast as seeds, but he always selected his favourite soaked currants from among grated cheese or any other food. Now that he was better able to fly and get up onto shelves to roost at night, I gave him the freedom of the woods and garden, in fact anywhere he cared to go. I hung his cage up above the badger compound against the wall next to the woods and beside my large aviary. At night he liked to return to it to roost, and he spent most of his time hopping about and perching on top of the wall, where he had a good view of his surroundings. Surprisingly, his favourite route to the woods was under the badger gate in the lower part of the wall. During heavy rain he would shelter beneath the stone wall and peep out through the wire mesh of the gate, just so that he could keep an eye on things in the garden, in case I arrived unexpectedly with the odd jar of grubs collected while gardening. Then he would slip below the gate and come fluttering up to me, chattering excitedly with expectation, and once more I thrust worms down his throat when he became tired of searching for his own food.

Gradually he became more proficient at grubbing for insects and worms. It gave me great pleasure to stroll about in the oak woods, where I had previously strolled with my badgers, while the blackbird flew low, stopping to investigate some old tree stump or ant heap and every now and then catching up with me. Then I would stop and rake quickly with a trowel among the leaves and sticks, while he jumped down and peered into the sweet-smelling leaf mould, picking up small spiders, wire worms and, on occasion, very large earthworms. He would become so excited that he nearly went frantic with his dancing and chattering, and I just could not clear the ground quickly enough. I had to look carefully where I was raking because his thin spindly feet were often right up against the trowel edge, and at times he came very near to having his toes injured.

His extremely sharp eyes enabled him to see the almost buried tip of a worm of grub, which he pecked and pulled to the surface. On one occasion he retrieved an earthworm the size of which I have never seen either before or since. Fully eight inches long and half an inch across its girth, it reminded me of a slow worm. The blackbird cut off one or two pieces by holding it in his beak, thrashing it from side to side, then finally taking the last long piece by the broken end with several jerks of the head, and tried to swallow it whole. By the time he came to the last swallow, the dark red point of the worm came stretching forth from between his mandibles, and he had to repeat his swallowing lest he should lose his great prize. As he swallowed the final bit with a stretch of his neck, his crop was so swollen and heaving with worm it was easy to see what difficulty he had in containing so great a specimen. He became unable to move from the spot where he found it, and with eyes closed he sank lower and lower until his legs were tucked up beneath him, exposing only the tips of his toes from under his soft mottled breast feathers. He roosted where he stood, while I returned to the cottage. But fifteen minutes later his crop was empty and he was awake and perky again, ever on the look-out for more food.

He always came fluttering to me if I went to his part of the garden, so I took to peeping from the upstairs windows to make sure he could find his way back to the wall from the woods. His eyesight was so good that even this practice became useless. He could recognize my shape in the window from away in the woods or beyond the garden hedge, up among the rocks and rough ground. I had not been in the window many seconds before he would appear from nowhere and come fluttering from wall to fence, to post and finally onto any ledge he could find next to the window, to sit there chirping loudly until I went out to him again.

I could have let him develop a very commanding personality, and he really would have led me up the proverbial garden path with his endless demands for attention and company. Gradually I ignored his calls, but always made sure he had a comfortable night's roosting place well out of harm's way before I went to bed. When he was completely independent he flew off in the opposite direction into the woods, his short tail and poorly feathered wing identifying him unmistakably. This was the last I saw of my entertaining feathered friend. I knew he had returned to the wild and needed me no longer.

The city blackbird faces a different hazard from his country cousin. He has to avoid that much-feared predator, man (not to mention his domestic pets). Most blackbirds are dark and not too conspicuous, and can usually conceal their nests from all but the keenest eye of boy or cat, but a pure white albino blackbird living in the busy surroundings of Liverpool University had little chance of survival.

The white blackbird was so conspicuous amongst the dark city buildings that, as she flew from building to building, or tree to tree, she showed like a pure white dove, particularly in the dull days of early spring, as she searched for a corner in which to build her nest. Finally she chose the window sill of the veterinary building in the University, much to the delight of the occupants. But she had not reckoned with those who walked and played in the city streets. She was soon spotted by the young city boys from a school nearby, and from then on, she was harried persistently, some boys playing truant from school to keep up the chase. The gang was determined to catch and kill her because of her whiteness. Only small shrubs concealed the window sill from the pavement and they were poor protection for her.

One of the staff appealed to the gardeners to help with defences and a barbed wire entanglement was erected around the nest. Even the University security staff were asked to keep an eye on the area as the young boys came both late at night and early in the morning. Had she been a golden eagle or osprey, not much more could have been done to protect her from these ten-year-olds. Many of the staff voluntarily worked late, because while the room was in use, the children dared not try to reach her, and under this protection she built her nest and laid her eggs.

The boys then redoubled their efforts, arriving at dawn, determined to press home their attack, and so the security patrol, the gardeners, the secretaries, the technicians and the vets extended their watch.

The incubation seemed endless, but finally the next hurdle was cleared and the young hatched successfully. Now the parents became even more conspicuous as they flew in and out of the nest with food for the young, and the children became more determined to catch her.

Early one morning disaster struck when the nest was found torn from its moorings. Some of the young were killed but some chicks were rescued. Despite valiant attempts by members of the staff to rear them, they too died.

But what of the white and beautiful parent? Had she been caught by the gang of children? To everyone's relief she was seen around the buildings again, already carrying nesting material to build herself a second nest. With no thought for her lost young, her instinct was once more to build with the indomitable determination of so many birds in the wild.

8

Young Hedgehogs:
Urchins of the Borran's Scrubland

The night was quiet as my daughter lay in bed, windows wide open in the still summer's night. An owl outside called in soft bubbling tones to her young owlet, as it sat waiting for the mouse or vole its mother would bring. Her young charge was making a continuous husky 'whoo-oo' like the hoot of an adult owl with laryngitis. The slightest sound seems magnified when the window is wide open and sleep is elusive. Suddenly a scream of some animal in pain rent the air, and Suzanne leapt from her bed and peered out to see what predator was causing such anguish to its prey. Although the stars were bright, there was no moon to throw light onto the drive, and nothing could be seen.

Late the next evening, Suzanne returned to the house to prepare a meal. Hardly had she reached the door when faint squealings were heard from the vegetation at the side of the drive, and although the light had almost faded she went in search of the young things, guided by their calls. As she parted the ferns, two tiny hedgehogs, the smallest and most pathetic creatures imaginable, their eyes not yet open, staggered out onto the drive, cold and hungry. Gathering them up, my daughter took them into the warmth of her kitchen. After all, these babies were too young to be away from the safety and comfort of their leafy nursery. So where was their mother?

Although she placed the hedgehogs in a cardboard box lined with woolly material, they were reluctant to lose the contact of hands and arms, which gave them the feel of the soft underside of their mother. Suzanne realized that the first requirement for her babies was warm milk and glucose, and with care and patience she persuaded them to take a few drops, holding them in her hands to provide the warmth and contact for which they craved. Once they were satisfied, she placed them in the box with a hot-water bottle wrapped in her scarf as a substitute for their mother, and they settled down to sleep for an hour or two.

Later Suzanne took a torch out into the garden to look for their nest, with a view to returning them to their mother. Instead she found yet a third little urchin crawling about on the drive, also squealing with cold and hunger. Suddenly she realized the meaning of the dreadful cry she had heard the previous night. Their mother had been killed by the fox which hunted the scrubland in the vast garden, the home of many small creatures such as rabbits, hedgehogs, mice and birds. It is a paradise for wildlife, an attractive hunting ground for the fox, and full of interest for the naturalist.

She took the third little hedgehog indoors, nursed and fed it and put it with the other two. They all nestled down happily together. But for how long, she wondered? They were small, and they would have to be fed a little and often. Through the long night Suzanne was up several times, heating their water bottle and giving them more drops of warm milk from the tip of a teaspoon, since nothing else was available to suit such unexpected visitors.

Work next day was an unpleasant thought for my daughter after her vigil by the hedgehog babies, so she called first thing in the morning, with 'Here you are, Mother, I know you love caring for young things. I'm worn out with my night of feeding and keeping them warm'. When I saw what she had brought me, I thought that at least I had not yet reared hedgehogs, and as they were so small, frail and in need of care the challenge was there. My immediate concern was to find something with which to feed them, their mouths being so small. At first I used an eye dropper. All my previous mammals had been large enough to suck from a small bottle with a teat.

By eleven o'clock they were struggling round their box, so I prepared a feed of warm milk, glucose and a little raw egg, and kept it warm by standing the cup in a bowl of hot water. To make a record of their future progress I took each one in turn and weighed it. Then I wrapped each in a towel, except for the head, and held it on my knee with one hand round the body and the other holding the eye dropper. I found that their eagerness to feed and their lack of teeth made the glass end of the dropper slide around in their mouths, causing most of the milk to come out of the side. I soon rectified this by supporting the glass tube of the dropper with the hand which held the baby, making it more rigid and enabling an even flow to be delivered from the bulb. Feeding was so slow and painstaking that the poor mites became more and more frustrated with the hard tip of the dropper. I had to devise some other method.

The rubber sac from a fountain pen, pierced with a pin and fitted to the end of the glass dropper, proved the most success-ful alternative. The little hedgehogs had something soft to suck, and they were less frustrated at feeding time. The babies, two males and one female, weighed $2\frac{1}{2}$ ounces each. They had a sparse coating of soft light-coloured spines and their legs and stomachs were naked. Of course their eyes had not yet begun to open.

After every feed I returned them to their box of dried leaves, which had now replaced the woolly material, so as to be more in keeping with their nest in the wild. The hot-water bottle underneath the box provided a gentle warmth, encouraging them to dig down and nestle into the bottom of the box. Once I had established a routine at feeding time, everything went well and they put on weight steadily at the rate of about three ounces a week, which was good, considering their original weight.

When they were about a fortnight old their eyes began to open, showing slight glimpses of light from among the hair which now covered their faces. This had a significant effect, as until then they had slept most of the time between feeds. But once their eyes were properly open, at about three weeks old, they started to move around in their box of leaves, explore each other and take some notice of their surroundings.

At four weeks old, when I started to wean them, they started to grow very lively and needed more exercise than the box could provide. Also they became uncomfortable to handle because their spines were no longer soft and supple in the hand, but were now numerous and sharp, growing out in every direction.

They were weaned like fox cubs on Farlene mixed with milk and egg, to which I added a very little scraped raw meat. When I cut down the frequency of feeds and introduced them to a spoon, feeding time became a messy business! I still held them in my hand on my knee on a towel, and put the spoon under their little snouts. Quite soon they learnt that they no longer had anything to suck, but had to shoot out their comparatively long tongues and lick out of the bowl of the spoon. How they enjoyed it once they had passed the sneezing and spluttering stage! It always surprises me how quickly animals learn to avoid the unpleasant part of getting the food up their noses. Of course, they needed a wipe with a damp cloth after each feed, as a small child needs his face washing after being taken down from his high chair.

Once they had learnt to lap up the food, I put the mixture on a shallow plate on newspaper on the floor, or better still, when fine, out on the lawn. They never learnt any table manners and I discovered that the shallow plate had many advantages. Kneeling over them to keep them out of the food was quite a business, as they always launched themselves straight into the middle, eating it as they went. But if all three did this together, there would be an appalling mess and wastage of food. So they had to be picked up constantly, with gloved hands, and replaced at the edge of the plate. I also learnt to have a shallow baking tin of warm water and a rough towel handy at the side while they were feeding. As soon as each one had eaten he was put in the tin of water to have a walk around to remove the food which was clinging to his coat, underside and feet. They enjoyed bathing in water, but to lift them out and gently rub them dry proved quite a fiddly business with so small a wriggling animal. The bedding of dried leaves on a folded newspaper was changed at every feed, and after each had been for a stroll and a sniff about the grass, all three were returned to the box until the next feed.

At this stage of their development their number was unexpectedly increased when another hedgehog was introduced to the family. One evening I decided to go out in the car to visit my local sett of badgers, which I had not seen for a couple of months. At dusk, driving down a busy road under trees with a footpath on one side, I suddenly spotted what looked like one of my baby hedgehogs, only smaller, running frantically down the gutter of the roadside. There was a lorry close behind me, so I indicated to him to overtake, and stopped as soon as it was safe. When I returned I found the little thing still running down the road, making no attempt to get onto the side. The kerb was fairly high at that spot, so no doubt it was unable to get away from the constant danger of traffic. Somehow it had become parted from its brothers and sisters, and lost. I could find no other hedgehogs in the rough ground to the side where I could return it, so I decided to wrap it in a duster and put it in the boot of the car until I had paid my visit to the badger sett.

A young creature should not be regarded as 'lost' too hastily, and I am always extremely careful before taking one home to rear. Only too often people say 'he was lost, so I took him home', and then find it more difficult to rear than they expected. They are quite unable to give either the time or the understanding which is needed to rear and return to the wild the particular animal which they have taken into their care, often quite unnecessarily. Young birds are particular victims of this so-called kindness, especially young owls and other birds of prey. Usually a short period of discreet observation will be sufficient to show that the parent bird knows quite well where her young are scattered and will come to them with food. Young deer and leverets are animals which are left by their parents until they return to feed them, and anybody finding one lying hidden on the ground should leave it undisturbed and untouched. Only if there are obvious signs of injury, and one is prepared to give a great deal of time and patience to the animal, should one interfere with nature and remove it into one's care for nursing.

The fourth little hedgehog, Stranger, though older than the three I already had, was less than half their weight having had to forage for its food in the wild. It had a slight infestation of fleas which was soon removed with a light dusting of dog flea powder.

Hedgehogs have quite a character and it was interesting to observe their behaviour with the newcomer in their midst. When I returned that night I prepared a meal for them all, and introduced the new arrival to the others at feeding time. All were placed round the plate of food, but Stranger had no idea what to do with it. It had been fed on natural food all its young life, and there could be difficulty at this stage in feeding it on anything else but worms and wild food. Yet I was anxious to put some weight on the little thing. Hedgehogs, when born in the latter half of the year, often die during the winter unless they have had the chance of a good supply of food and put on the layer of fat which is essential for survival during the winter hibernation.

I allowed the newcomer to roam round while the trio fed and bathed, as I wished to concentrate on it alone and do my best to get some food into this wild one. I chopped a few worms and put some on the surface of the Farlene, egg and raw meat to encourage it to feed. An animal already living on wild food should not need artificial nourishment, but as it was so under-sized, its weight could be increased more quickly artificially, although it would have to be taught to revert to its natural diet before release. Once it acquired the taste of Farlene, milk and egg with the worms, it tucked into the mixture with pleasure and progressed rapidly in weight and general development.

After feeding, all four hedgehogs were put back into their box of dried leaves for the night, with its side open to allow them to crawl out and about on the newspaper-covered floor. I had discontinued the hot-water bottle at weaning time. Not only were they moving about more freely but they were not showing any signs of clinging to the warmth, and would curl up to sleep anywhere in the box.

The original trio were in bed before Stranger arrived. It sniffed vigorously among the leaves and also at the three little bodies already settled down to rest. This had a decidedly disturbing effect on the trio. They rose and seemed to agree that this intruder must be pushed out as quickly as possible. Sniffing it all over with their snouts from a position at the rear of the box, they pushed him towards the entrance. As it neared the door the little hedgehog tried running round to the back again, and a general chase ensued. Stranger was eventually ejected and the three settled down once more in the leaves to sleep. The pathetic little one wandered round on the newspaper, but found nowhere to settle so it waited until the others were sound asleep and then later crept back into the box, round the three prickly little bundles and finally settled down behind them all at the back of the box.

In the morning they were all four asleep together, but by the mess among the newspaper, there must have been much activity during the night. The box contained not only leaves, but was a jumble of torn and crumpled newspapers which they had been busily shredding and taking in as extra bedding. It was amazing to watch them at this household chore. They were so small in size, yet handled and carried large sections of paper in their mouths.

As I have mentioned, their spines became quite dense and hardened at about five weeks old, making them difficult to handle. I was surprised to find how young they were when they developed their defensive instinct of drawing their spines up and over forward; and when the prickles stood on end, they criss-crossed in every direction. The earliest sign of reaction took place at about three weeks old, when the spines above the hair line on the face, instead of lying backwards as I approached, came forwards like an old man frowning.

It helped to use two hands to pick them up. The fingers could be tucked down the sides and curled into the soft spineless stomach. Then they could be rolled over into the cupped hand, filling it comfortably like a tennis ball, though it could be rather painful if one's hand was clenched. This was an excellent way to inspect the underside of the hedgehog. Unless very alarmed it did not curl up completely, revealing its little face and nose like a crumpled currant and four tiny feet with long sharp claws and minute little pads.

Also, at the same early age, they performed the peculiar behaviour of self-anointing. This they did by drawing their heads over their backs and assuming a most contorted posture, the legs on one side raised, and falling over sideways onto their backs. The long slim tongue goes in and out quite quickly as they lather their spines over with bubbly saliva. This strange behaviour appears to be triggered off by chewing something unusual like wood, the leather strap on a sandal, or even a slug before they have become used to the flavour. There are several explanations for this performance. One, for example, is that it is to remove fleas from between the spines or to give themselves some sort of camouflage scent in the same way that a dog will roll on a decaying animal.

During the several weeks I nursed them, they were introduced to more and more of the garden, to forage for the food of their choice, while I watched to see which items they preferred and which they rejected. Those which they chose, as well as many earthworms, were collected and fed to them, enabling them to eat many more than they would have obtained by hunting among the vegetation on their own. Milk, Farlene and raw egg were still given at the recognized feeding times.

I was interested to note that, if I set down their box of leaves in the same place in the garden and let them walk out at their own free will, rather than lifting them out onto the grass, they would run away from it quite quickly in any direction, but that during their foraging they would gradually work their way round and back into the box again. By the speed at which they went away, it seemed certain they would be lost among the rockery or down near the pool, and though tempted at first to gather them up straight away I was relieved to find that they all returned to the box. When they were about six weeks old, weighed over twelve ounces and were feeding well in the wild, the time came to return them to the rough scrubland in which they were born.

My daughter constructed a fox-proof wooden shelter filled with leaves in her garden, under cover of brambles inside a large compound of wire netting. Within the perimeter were trees, shrubs, and rough tussocky grass, and one day at the end of the summer we transferred them to the wooden shelter. That evening, as the sun set and night was falling, one by one the four little hedgehogs trooped out for their nightly foraging. What a wonderful surprise for them! Instead of the newspaper covered floor of their artificial habitat, they were at last to spend a night amid some of the most delightful smells and sounds for which any hog could have wished. A hedgehog's eyesight is very limited but it has a strong sense of smell, and the four were soon rooting and snorting and snuffling among the leaves and bramble as though they were experienced old hands at searching for their food.

Stranger was much smaller than the original three, but although it had been artificially fed for a short time, it was much more experienced than its step-sister and brothers, and was much more adept at finding small grubs down in the rough ground.

We put out their saucer of Farlene and milk, so that at least they would not go hungry, though now they must search for their protein food themselves. My daughter also collected slugs from her vegetable garden and put them in their compound. No doubt she hoped to give them the flavour of these delicacies so that they would play their part, when completely free, in ridding her of these pests in return for their keep!

After a week, my daughter summoned us to the grand opening of the wire fence to watch what happened when the hedgehogs realized that they were no longer contained. Just before dusk we went round rolling up the netting and removing all the supporting sticks. As usual they trooped out to the familiar feeding area and found their dish, which was several yards from the sleeping quarters. They walked about in it when they ate, as they always did, and then went in search of those fat black, brown, or cream-coloured slugs which abound in plenty there, some as much as five inches long. When the most experienced hedgehog reached the usual boundary, it seemed suddenly to notice that there was no netting and set off at a tremendous pace away into the thicket. This gave the signal to the others, for they too ran off on their short little legs, their bodies raised up off the ground as high as their legs could lift them. Stranger never came back but the other three returned nightly for the food put out for them near the wooden sleeping box, and for several weeks two returned to sleep by day until they found alternative accommodation.

Neighbours of my daughter, who had been so interested in their development and subsequent return to the wild, frequently came to her with much pleasure saying 'I am sure it was one of your little hedgehogs which visited my garden last evening'. Unfortunately we did not mark them, but we like to think it was.

9

Barn Owls:
Ghosts in the Gloaming

Above the dusky roughland in the cool of a summer twilight, the barn owl (*Tyto alba*) could be seen drifting noiselessly like a phantom, in search of mammals in the undergrowth. Sitting underneath a large oak tree I watched her ghostly movements as she paused occasionally, suspended on white wings, her long white knock-kneed legs dangling down ready to drop on a small vole in the grass. Down she pounced with partly folded wings, and gripped the tiny creature in her powerful talons until it was still. By a deft stroke of her beak she crushed its skull and, with two or three gulps, swallowed it whole.

Rising again on long pale wings, using her keen ears and eyes, she silently quartered the field. I could see the delicate orange and pearl-grey back and head, faintly barred tail and pure white breast, while her heart-shaped face with dark almond eyes turned this way and that scanning the herbage below. As she approached, without seeing me, she passed close by in her slow flight, turned her head and, with a look of disdain, stared straight at me down her 'nose' before winging her way past me up the field and over the hedge to her next hunting ground.

She lived not far away in an old barn. From the barn owl's association with ancient buildings and churches, and its wheezy snoring in the roost and wild shriek on the wing, it is not difficult to see why it used to be considered haunting and evil, especially when it hunted around the graves in a churchyard.

Many barn owls are killed on motorways and other fast roads; pesticides have already reduced their numbers, and suitable nest sites and habitats are diminishing with changed farming methods, so that the barn owl is now a species much in need of care and help. The Protection of Birds Act does include the barn owl in the First Schedule, giving the maximum legal protection and even prohibiting photography at the nest without a permit, but even so everyone must do all they can to encourage this useful and attractive bird.

All birds of prey and their eggs are protected under the 1954 and 1967 Acts, and a person possessing such a bird which has been taken within the previous six months is liable to prosecution unless he has a licence. A bird can only be kept without a licence if it is disabled, or if it can be proved by close ringing to have been bred in captivity. In the case of an injured bird, it must be released back into the wild as soon as it is well again.

During one cold February night a beautiful mature female barn owl on a hunting foray was fanning over the fields at dusk, coming to rest on the roadside fencing posts to stand and watch for vole movements in the grass verge. Finding nothing she drifted low across the busy carriageway and was struck by a car that left her to flounder on the grass at the side until picked up next day and taken along to my veterinary surgeon. This was how I received my first injured barn owl, Beauty.

Under anaesthetic the vet took an X-ray photograph which showed that this magnificent white owl had fractured the humerus in one wing and had another fracture in the other wing at the top of the humerus, almost in the joint. The first fracture was set and pinned, and I took the bird into the accommodation I kept ready for such a patient. I nursed her for four weeks until the pin could be removed safely. The second wing was much more difficult as the fracture was almost compounded and was right at the joint. Drilling and wiring the bone was considered but rejected. Although the tendons and muscles were in good condition, it was thought that more harm might result if these were damaged in any way. The barn owl's slow laboured wing beat, as it flies low over the ground, was also taken into consideration in deciding to leave this wing. Our hope was that further confinement yet with some movement but no strain would be beneficial.

Fortunately Beauty was a keen feeder during her confinement, so her general condition was good and she made an admirable patient. She was kept in the cage in the utility room where it was not only warm but, most important, she could become used to the movement of human beings near her cage. In this way she learnt not to flush and damage herself when I approached, as she would have done if the cage had been placed away from all activity. Injured wild creatures must develop sufficient confidence and become accustomed to human contact, to avoid stress when essential handling or cleaning has to be done.

Occasionally Beauty was in no mood for disturbance and snorted at my approach making a sound like a football bladder being deflated. At the same time she would crouch down with wings outspread and sway from side to side lowering her head until it brushed the perch, then lift it in a large arc up and down again. Had I persisted, her next attitude of threat would have been to hurl herself onto her back and strike out with her claws, clacking loudly all the time with her tongue. Rather than cause distress on these occasions, I would leave her for several minutes. When I approached her once again, she would be quite unconcerned, standing up very tall and slim in her K-legged attitude with eyes closed and carefree. I never discovered what caused the rapid change in mood.

I was able, by keeping her nursing cage nearby, to observe her every movement. Hunger seemed to strike about mid-day and often she would stir from her roost in the darkest corner of the cage and step down off her perch, waddle across to a dead mouse, pick it up and, without turning it round in her claws and beak in the usual manner, just swallow it whole. If I heard her moving in her cage and peeped round the door, she immediately took on a superior air, looking at me with her dark oriental eyes and an almost human expression, as though she wondered why I had come to watch the perfectly normal business of eating a mouse. After staring at me for several seconds she would begin to sway and snort in a threatening manner, so I would simply take the hint and leave her to herself.

Beauty was a very co-operative patient while in her nursing cage, and we became quite used to her living so near to us. On the first of March the great day came to remove the pin in her wing and to check progress by X-ray. The pinned wing had healed beautifully, but the other wing was still very doubtful, so she was kept indoors until the frosty nights were over. A fortnight later she was transferred to the large summerhouse, now transformed into a second aviary for this important patient. I fixed a tea-chest in one corner with perches at various heights to enable her to hop up and get inside, since she could not, of course, fly. She really enjoyed an old sloping ladder at the other side as it provided roosting places on many levels, and she could get up and down from rung to rung easily, to collect the food on the floor.

For the next few weeks we had our problems with her, and although she had the excercise she needed for her wings, she had several heavy falls. One or two stomach upsets made visits from Brian Coles necessary to give her the required injections, and on the first of May she had another X-ray since she should have been flying after five weeks in the aviary.

The shoulder joint was causing trouble, as occasionally the wing rotated when she was on the floor in the threat posture, and she was unable to fold it to her side. Another operation was performed, though by now we had reluctantly come to the conclusion that she never would be able to go free. But she was an otherwise healthy and very beautiful barn owl. So what was her future to be?

I had heard of one or two people in different parts of the country who also had injured barn owls which could not be freed, and I wondered if there was any possibility of getting a mate for her. It was quite unthinkable to consider putting down such a beautiful and rare bird on whom so much time, patience and skill had been spent by my conscientious vet. If she was to stay with me for care and attention I could not consider letting her live in solitary confinement, so in July I got in touch with June Garbutt of Kirkby Stephen, who has had long experience of keeping injured barn owls.

She knows my wildlife work and immediately offered help. Not long after, she rang me to say that her injured breeding female barn owl had died, leaving the injured male, Kirk, without a partner. Like me, June does not believe in keeping any fit creature in captivity; she only keeps injured birds in her aviaries, if possible as breeding pairs, putting their offspring into the wild.

Although I assumed that Beauty was a female, I was not absolutely sure, but I knew the behaviour of the male would solve that problem. For a couple of nights Kirk was kept in his cage inside the aviary while my owl came down to investigate. No signs of quarrelling took place, so the cage door was opened and they were left on their own for the night. Next morning I was delighted to see them roosting together on the top rung of the ladder, although I noticed that Kirk, also injured in the same wing, had more difficulty getting around. The friendship developed and as they often roosted tightly pressed together by day, I was convinced they were a pair. Now I began to study the subtle differences in their plumage. Admittedly there was very little to distinguish between them, but there was just that much difference to give me the clue to sexing all the other barn owls I have since reared.

At the end of July I was presented with a young male barn owl named Peck, with a strained left wing and unable to fly, so again I had an occupant for my nursing cage. He progressed well and was about ready for transfer to the large aviary when trouble struck.

While I was making one of my frequent checks on him in his cage, I noticed the walls were spattered with blood, but at a glance could see no damage to the bird. Peck was standing on his perch looking his usual self and, as the blood was dry, it was clear that he had done something in the night. I suspected that he had been eating a fresh mouse and had flicked small pieces of it about as birds of prey often do, but I continued to inspect him at half hour intervals during the day. On one such visit I caught him in the act of what can only be called an attempted suicide. He was pecking under his left wing making an open wound from which blood was spurting. I took him at once to Brian's surgery where, as soon as I removed the cotton wool from the wound, the blood welled up like a small spring. Despite the spurting blood and messy plumage the vet managed to find the puncture, stitched it, and so arrested the bleeding. Birds have very little blood to lose and Peck was so weak he could not stand. Laying him across his hand Brian said, without conviction, 'I hope he's going to be all right.' He covered the wound with a pad of cotton wool and strapped the wing lightly against the body to prevent him pecking it.

Back at home, Peck was too weak to be put out in his cage, so I contained him for the night on a bed of hay in a cardboard box on top of the boiler and administered glucose and water. Always hopeful, I also popped a dead mouse into the box in case he recovered sufficiently during the night. Much to my relief he was on his feet by daybreak and looking more like himself again. On the fourth day the strapping was removed and the injury painted with gentian violet to inhibit pecking. The stitches were never removed.

Once again I was amazed at Brian's skill in being able in all that mess to find, stitch and successfully join the severed ends of the artery without stopping the blood supply to the wing. This unexpected incident illustrates the sort of setback that can occur when a patient is progressing well, and one simply cannot assume total success until the bird is back on the wing in the wild and known to be hunting for itself.

Peck made a full recovery and in September I collected a young mate called Guttata, for him. This was one of the dark-breasted barn owls bred in captivity by Caroline Hunt, who wished to have her owl trained and returned to the wild. Caroline's golden owl and my white one settled down well together in my aviary, where I kept them through the winter as they developed powerful flight and learnt to kill their own food. Contrary to expectations, Caroline's captive-bred bird was far more timid than my wild one, and as soon as I appeared round the corner of the cottage Guttata would dive for cover inside the tea-chest roost and stay there for some time.

Peck and Guttata became quite vociferous after dark, snoring and calling loudly as they flew up and down the thirty foot aviary. One night, to my surprise, I saw a wild barn owl sitting on an overhanging branch of an ash tree having come in answer to their calls. Little did I know we had barn owls in the area. When the wild one saw me it flew off along the hedges of the field screeching so loudly that I could still hear it flying along the far edge of the large pasture. It returned once more to the garden where I watched it for several seconds before it departed for good, shrieking as it went. Tawny owls often visit their captive species, but never before had I seen barn owls doing the same.

When winter was nearly over I had thoughts of breeding with my first injured pair, Beauty and Kirk, and releasing the two youngsters, Peck and Guttata, from a farmer friend's barn in a valley in Cumbria. I noticed, though, that by now Caroline's owl often never left the tea-chest at dusk, but crouched at the back like a golden feather tea-cosy, while by day the male stood outside to roost instead of sharing the box with his mate. Surely, I wondered, Caroline's golden *Tyto alba guttata* was not contemplating laying! I had made no preparations for them to breed, intending them to go to the barn. Days and weeks went by but, not wishing to disturb them, I left them alone until the maximum time for incubation had passed. Then gently pushing her to one side I saw four white eggs in the sawdust tray on which she was sitting. As the chest had not been prepared for breeding, the tray was still there and I found four eggs behind it as well. So they had tried really hard.

Examination revealed them all to be infertile but in case Guttata was preparing to lay again, I rang up the farmer, John Webster, to see if I could bring the owls up to his prepared barn immediately. As it was still only April there was a slight chance of a second clutch, though eight was a big clutch for the young bird. The free-standing stone barn stood about a quarter of a mile from the rest of the farm buildings, high up on the rough sheep pasture. The situation was ideal for barn owls with excellent hunting territory on the rough land stretching twenty miles or so over the Howgill Fells, while on the lower side the land dropped down into the wide river valley with pasture and hay fields and many old stone buildings dotted along its length. On such undisturbed ground, short-tailed voles and shrews were plentiful, as was indicated by the successful breeding of short-eared owls and kestrels, for whom these are the staple food.

John Webster, the owner, who farms the land himself, is particularly interested in all forms of wildlife. In 1973, following a study of the mammal contents of barn owl pellets during 1969 and 1970, his paper 'Seasonal Variations in Mammal

Contents of Barn Owl Castings' was published. This showed that without doubt the natural food preference of the barn owl is the short-tailed vole, and provided a ready means of determining when a released owl was feeding normally.

He is always keen to establish barn owls on his farm, and had already constructed an excellent breeding box high up in the roof of this solitary stone barn, which, with its ventilation slits and beams, provided the ideal surroundings from which to introduce these two young barn owls into the wild.

We took the owls Peck and Guttata up the hillside in a cardboard box, into what seemed a black interior, but our eyes soon became accustomed to the light and we saw that John had already put down some dead chicks and mice and a shallow bowl of water in which they could bath. We released the owls separately and it was a great joy to see Peck spread his large white wings in heraldic attitude as he flew upwards, coming to rest on the flat top of the drystone barn wall under the slope of the roof. Guttata remained on the floor with her usual threatening display.

For about two weeks they were confined to the barn. The large door was left open and the aperture covered with wire netting to let the owls familiarize themselves with part of the vast stretches of surrounding grassland, while the ventilation slits were blocked temporarily with balls of hay. The floor of the barn was on two levels. The lower floor some ten feet below was divided; part, approached by a small separate door, was enclosed for wintering cattle, the remaining two levels contained some hay and were accessible to the owls.

For the first five days, dead day-old chicks were provided, supplemented by the wild mice which frequented the building. Peck and Guttata had already received special training in catching and killing live prey, so they knew exactly what to do when they saw mice in the barn. For a few days from 3 May all chick feeding was discontinued, and dead mice were provided nightly from the stock which I had bred. This was later followed by a few nights with live mice until on 13 May the top part of the large netted door was opened.

The next day Peck was seen in the barn during the afternoon when he hopped up into the nest box under the roof. At

9.45 p.m. Guttata was perched on top of the door, and at 10 o'clock the white owl could clearly be seen hunting in a pasture field beside the farmhouse and along the edge of a larch plantation. On 15 May Peck was observed just before 10 p.m., hunting in the large garth to the east of the farmhouse, and then up into the adjoining farmer's pasture, disappearing southwards towards the ghyll.

Until the owls became completely self-supporting, about half a dozen dead mice were left inside the barn at night. One of the owls, possibly Peck, was seen in the barn as it flew up into the nest box. Two days later, two out of three mice had been taken and the darker owl was seen to fly from a beam into the nest box. This confirmed that both owls were still returning to the barn to roost by day, and that they were depending less on the mice provided.

On 20 May at 11.10 p.m. when the farmer and his wife were returning along the narrow lane to the house, they saw in the headlights the white owl on the track in front of them some three quarters of a mile from the farm. They pulled up and watched him for a long time in the lights before he flew off along the lane and over the hedge, disappearing towards the lower meadows. The next afternoon John was pleased to see he had returned to the barn and was roosting there for the day. This sighting indicated how quickly the owls were extending their territory yet still returning to the barn to roost.

A week later, the white owl was no longer roosting in the barn, but the dark one was seen on several dates, perched near the owl box. The last definite sighting in the barn was on 1 June. Her behaviour was similar on all these occasions. On hearing the sound of John's entry into the lower part of the barn, she would hop into the box. Quite often he heard nothing but the sound of her claws scratching on the box as she moved inside.

After 27 June no further sightings were made of either bird, but John very kindly collected up all the owl castings found inside the barn. On analysis, they were found to contain bird bones (chicks), captive bred mouse skulls (*Mus musculus*), some common shrew skulls (*Sorex araneus castaneus*), and two castings contained the skulls of short-tailed voles (*Microtus agrestic hirtus*), which proved conclusively that at least one of the owls

—almost certainly Peck—was taking wild prey. Previous research determined that the most usual and commonly taken prey species of the barn owl are the common shrew and short-tailed vole, and though these owls had been fed on mice and had hunted along the plantation where woodmice live, on release they immediately fell into the normal prey choice of the wild barn owl. As John says, this begs the interesting question, 'By which sense do predators choose their prey?'

Meanwhile in May my husband and I returned to the New Forest to continue some field work we had been doing the previous year. By now my injured owls, Beauty and Kirk, had quite settled in their tea-chest, which had been erected in the aviary in early January in case they wanted to breed. All spring they had shown no signs of breeding, and I had made arrangements for them to spend the holiday in Terry Well's large garden shed with attached aviary.

A few days before our departure, I helped Terry to make their temporary home as nearly like their own aviary as possible, As cripples, they needed to know their way around the ladders which led to the nest box. Terry had never had barn owls before, though he had reared many birds, and was delighted to have them to look after and study. He was prepared for advice and help, and readily took my suggestions for their well-being. Like most owls they are static and uninteresting by day, sitting like K-legged statues, their eyes closed and motionless, so I wondered if he really would find them of sufficient interest.

As I lifted each one in turn into the carrying box for transfer to their new home, I was surprised and shocked to find in the peat which covered the floor of their tea-chest, a single pure white almost spherical egg! Was I to cancel my visit to the New Forest or, since this was only the first egg, wrap it in cotton wool in a polystyrene box to keep it warm, and take it along with the owls? I decided on the latter course, and when I arrived with owls and egg Terry was as surprised as I had been. We felt there was a chance that Beauty might lay more when she had settled down.

I put the single egg inside the long tunnel-shaped nesting area in his shed, and popped each owl in after it. They quickly

Peck in the heraldic attitude; and hunting

Guttata in the threat position

Avis, Alba and Almond as youngsters

and noisily shuffled along to the furthest end, huddling down in a corner in complete darkness. A few dead chicks and mice were provided in a position similar to that in their own aviary, and the door was shut to leave them in peace until the next day, when I visited the aviary again to check that they had settled in. The most encouraging sign was that they were feeding successfully, using their ladder to reach the chicks. I departed to the New Forest knowing they were in good hands.

Mid-May saw encouraging signs which could mean more laying and, like Caroline's Guttata, my injured female, Beauty, seldom left the nest for food but spent her whole time huddled down in the dark depths of the nest box. Terry had no means of knowing how many eggs there were, as he felt it most important to leave the birds in peace.

The incubation of the eggs of birds of prey begins as soon as they are laid; so, from thirty to thirty five days later, hatching takes place at two or three day intervals, making quite a range of ages in a clutch of young barn owls. Towards the likely incubation day of the first youngster, the parents were fed as usual on day old chicks, but now stripped of their heads and feet, so that there could be no confusion in the adults' minds between their own scraggy little offspring and the food. Experience shows that barn owls are prone to eat their young when breeding in captivity.

Exciting, strange sounds were coming from the nest box by the third week in June, but still Terry was not letting his curiosity get the better of him and he refrained from opening it. He recorded the date on which the first sound was heard, but he deferred any action until our return from our trip south. Wisely he increased the number of food chicks and added a pinch of vitamins to the day's supply. The sounds made by the newly hatched were intermittent, and Terry found no way of describing the noise, only that it was different from anything he had heard before and he was sure it was not made by the parents.

The voice of the young around the time of hatching is described by my colleague, Tony Warburton, who has bred many barn owls, as a chittering noise, especially when left by the hen. They also hiss very faintly. He mentions that owlets still in the egg will answer the calls of their hatched brothers and sisters as much as one or two days before their own birth. Tony described the owlets at hatching as approximately two inches in length, grotesque in appearance, having large heads with closed bulbous eyes. The beak is long and vulture-like, and their pink-skinned pot-bellied bodies are lightly covered with a dirty white down, with bare patches on the sides of the neck and sparse down on the belly. Their legs are ill-developed and are of little use to them for the first few days.

Terry reported that the voices of more than one young owlet were heard, so we decided to explore the nest box carefully a week or so later. When we removed both parents, we saw that Beauty's breast was stained with peat on which she brooded her eggs, and there was one quite plump owlet, Avis, followed by two smaller ones, which I named Alba and Almond, in varying stages of growth. They really were the ugliest babies I had ever seen. Most young things are more attractive than their parents. This is certainly not true of the chicks of predatory birds.

Close ringing is best carried out at about eighteen days old, but with such a variation in size it meant disturbing them three times. The ring, supplied by the Hawk Trust, was slipped onto the leg of the eighteen-day-old Avis, and the younger two were ringed as they reached this age. The three of them were photographed out of the nest, so that a study of relative sizes and ages could be made. Alba seemed unable to stand, his eyes barely opening as he peered round, clacking his tongue in threat. The youngest, Almond, was red and so small, weak and floppy that I considered its chances of survival poor.

Terry, to his great credit, managed to provide food for the parents to give to their three offspring, and by the time the chicks were five weeks old a remarkable transformation had taken place. All three, Avis, Alba and Almond, were on their feet, growing larger every day, and covered with a white fluffy down. The facial discs of the eldest were showing well. By August their appearance had changed still further and they all had their white heart-shaped facial discs and dark oriental eyes. They were now shedding their down, covering the nest box and aviary with fluff as they flapped their wings, their primary feathers fully grown, and golden and grey mantled feathers cloaking their backs and wings.

Slight signs of dispute over food were observed as they still roosted in the nest; they were not yet quite old enough to perch outside its confines.

These barn owls were now nearly as large as their parents. Mutual preening took place, and their incessant hissing calls for food became very loud when they felt neglected or particularly hungry. The strain on the injured parents must have been considerable as they completed the task of feeding this large family. Barn owls are very slow developers compared to tawny owls. At the time that barn owl chicks are just shedding their white down, a tawny owl would be fully feathered with juvenile plumage and leaving the nest for good.

By the end of August the three owlets were fully feathered and able to fly. Their mother was looking tired and often roosted away from her young, who also selected roosting places outside the nest. It was time for separation, because at this stage parents have been known to attack and even kill their young, who are now almost adults and competitors in the parents' territory. In the wild this danger does not occur as the young are easily driven out of the territory.

Avis, Alba and Almond, now in their own aviary, were introduced to live prey and their training began in earnest. Each owlet in turn was given a night on its own in the training aviary, while the other two spent the night in the larger flight. This enabled me to make sure that each was capable of catching and swiftly killing its own live food. Had they all been trained together I would have had little idea of their individual capabilities, and there was always the possibility that the less efficient would become lazy and depend on one of the others to kill for it.

Food training was complete by November, and they were fitted with British Trust for Ornithology (B.T.O.) rings and taken to two ready prepared barns. Avis and Alba—the eldest female and male—were taken up to John Webster's stone barn, where the earlier couple, Peck and Guttata, had lived for a few months during the previous summer. The barn provided plenty of exercise when they settled in. They always roosted in their prepared tea-chest nest box up in the apex of the roof and fed on dead chicks and mice.

If a barn owl is just placed in a barn by day without shutting it in with a full supply of food, it will fly out at dusk and possibly never return. Careful preparation is necessary if it is to remain in the barn. But it is well worth the effort. Apart from retaining them over their first winter when young barn owls are so vulnerable and until the food supply in the wild is plentiful and the weather good, a safe barn also helps them to become established, with a nest box, in peace and quiet, in the hope that they might breed in the spring.

This operation needs a co-operative farmer, who will not only give over the barn to the owls for their first season, but go to quite a deal of trouble sealing off every crack and cranny and ventilation slit, and covering over the door opening and any windows with wire netting to allow the owls to look out and take stock of their surrounding territory. Once breeding starts and four weeks after the young owlets are first heard in the nest box, all apertures to the outside world must be opened to allow the parents to fly in and out with wild food from the fields with which to feed their young. At the same time, some food such as dead chicks and mice must still be placed on the barn floor to supplement the diet, until they are no longer taken.

It is of great importance that *all* openings to the barn should be cleared of obstructions because the owls will never yet have seen their home from the outside, so may fail to find the opening through which they left, and other entrances are required to enable them to return to their young. On one occasion a farmer opened up only one ventilation slit out of several on the walls and left the door closed. In consequence, the male who went out early in the evening to fetch food for his mate, could not find his way back inside, eventually gave up trying and left the area. As he did not return, the female left her four youngsters and went out hunting on her own, and she too failed to find the tiny opening back into the barn. Two days later she was seen roosting outside the door where she could see inside the barn but could not get to her young. By the time this was discovered and the door opened to enable her to return, the two eldest chicks had, in their hunger, consumed their younger brother and sister, and the mother bird was left to feed and rear her two remaining offspring single-handed.

The third of my captive-bred barn owls, Almond, was taken down to an ancient brick and timber barn in Shropshire, and also provided with a deep dark nesting box. The area around her home was perfect barn owl territory, rough agricultural land with good hedgerows and banks and, above all, situated in a valley with no through road. Several barn owls had been seen at dusk hunting in the valley fields, and I hoped that a wild one would ultimately partner her. But in the meantime Almond lived on her own in my friend's barn, roosting by day down the tunnel of her box.

The New Year of 1976 began with some of the worst gales this country has ever known. The lakeland barn with Avis and and Alba held up well and no slates were blown off in spite of its bleak situation up on the hillside; but the brick barn in Shropshire lost a patch of tiles from its roof. At dawn—thankfully when the wind had slightly abated—Almond made her exit and took to the unwelcoming world of the wild. Her owner felt some concern for her wellbeing, but I knew her ability to catch any prey that moved and was less worried. Moreover, she went out at dawn after a night's food when the worst of the storm was over.

Barn owls, with their large soft wings, are very susceptible to strong winds. They are easily tossed and tumbled. Tony Warburton saw one blown off a fencing post from which it was hunting, and bowled over and over on the ground like an open newspaper. Severe snow and frosty winters are a danger to these owls as they have little residual fat on which to live. Their prey, the short-tailed vole, feeds and moves under the blanket of snow undetected by the owl which, if unable to find food, will die after only four or five days. Even very wet weather can present a problem as the barn owl is not able to keep its plumage dry during long exposures to rain. Its plumage is only partially weather-proof and so prolonged rain can make hunting impossible. The barn owl's habit of spending most of its time in buildings or under cover probably accounts for the lack of water resistance in its feathers.

Previously, a barn owl had been seen on several occasions in the vicinity of the Shropshire barn, standing on the fencing posts, watching and listening for vole movements in the hedgerow and verges, crossing the lane backwards and forwards low on white wings. To our great joy we also saw our ringed female, Almond, hunting in the valley one cold clear night after her release. In the words of my naturalist friend Michael Houston, writing in his Countryside column in the *Westmorland Gazette*, she was floating on 'ochre snow-flake wings beneath a silver moon in a pale white winter sky' — a perfect description of my beautiful and ghost-like bird of prey.

This Shropshire youngster, Almond, did find a partner, and although they never returned to the barn, both were seen over twelve months later hunting along the hedgerows and ditches of the valley, criss-crossing the tiny country lane. When she rested on a fence the two rings on her legs could be easily distinguished.

Meanwhile, in June, Avis and Alba, the pair in John Webster's barn, had produced two young. After the barn was opened up to the outside world, they were fed by their parents on voles and shrews from the wild and developed well, both in size and voice. On several occasions we sat motionless in the darkness of the barn, not only to watch but also to tape record the return of the male parent bird with food for his growing family. The young hissed and chittered with impatience when Alba passed the food over to Avis and she in turn tore it up and gave it to her offspring.

As the weeks went by, the young owls grew from strength to strength. They left the nest box and sat around in the barn, and although they were still fed by their parents, by now their food was not torn up for them but merely left on the landing board where they could come and feed themselves.

The summer of 1976 proved to be the longest dry summer on record. The rough grass above the barn became parched, and as the short-tailed vole population declined, shrews, which feed on the new grass shoots under the rank vegetation, became the main food for the growing owlets.

The end of July and early August saw the whole family out and about at dusk, standing on stone walls, gate posts and farming implements, now and again giving delight to us, hidden behind a wall, as they flew low over the ground on large white wings in their floppy laboured flight.

By the end of the month they still returned to the barn to roost by day, so John Webster was able to examine the regurgitated pellets picked up from below their perching places. Analysis revealed that the owls were having increasing difficulty in finding food in the dry ground, where the common shrew and pygmy shrews (*Sorex minutus*) were all that they could find, whereas in previous years the rough grazing around the barn had been well populated with short-tailed voles. Shortly afterwards the whole owl family disappeared from the area. No doubt they had departed in search of richer hunting grounds.

To the many people who enjoyed the long, uninterrupted sunshine this might not seem of much interest and concern, but to the owls that depend on voles for food it was of vital importance. The prolonged drought proved disastrous for this already declining and valuable species.

The barn owl population has recovered slightly in the past ten years since the severe decline caused by pesticides, but its existence is still precarious. In the *Atlas of Breeding Birds in Britain and Ireland*, the barn owl is recorded as breeding in almost every ten kilometre square of the country, which might suggest that as a species it is flourishing. Unfortunately, many hazards still remain.

The drought did not break in our area until October, and although barn owl parents frequently leave the home site on the completion of their breeding season, I was concerned that from the beginning of September there were no youngsters around the barn. Two months after the last sighting of the adult female, Avis, in her breeding ground, she was seen some ten miles south, lying injured on the carriageway of the M6 motorway near the Killington intersection. She must have given up hunting the valleys and flown over the passes of the Howgill Fells until she came out eventually onto the motorway. There she flew in a southerly direction, searching the long uncut banks which are the valuable haunts of many small mammals and, consequently, of the wind-hovering kestrel. In her search for food Avis collided with one of the many hazards invented by man—the motor car. Within yards of where she was found floundering in the grass, there was the dead body of a second barn owl. Was that her partner, Alba, or perhaps one of the youngsters from her nest?

She was in a bad state when a car driver picked her up and took her to the Kendal branch of the R.S.P.C.A. She was given to a local girl interested in birds, who took her to a veterinary surgeon, the late Michael Harkness, in Sedbergh. He rang up to consult Colin Armitstead, an experienced naturalist and authorized bird ringer, who was a friend of his and, coincidentally, of mine. Colin got in touch with me to say that Mike Harkness had just received an injured barn owl and asked if it was anything to do with me. As I had not placed any barn owls in the Sedbergh area my first reaction was that it could not be, but when he mentioned that it had a ring on each leg, and that one was a closed Hawk Trust ring, I exclaimed with horror that it must be Avis or Alba, one of my breeding pair from John Webster's barn in the Gaisgill area. Colin brought it over and a check of the ring number confirmed that it was indeed Avis. Tragically, she was back in my care just twelve months after she had first been put in John's barn.

We hoped that with skilled treatment and nursing Avis could learn to fly again as so many had done before. I rang the surgery to say that I was bringing a very important injured barn owl, and as soon as I arrived Brian took her straight into into the operating theatre. The poor creature was thin and bedraggled, worn out by her struggle for survival among the grimy roadside vegetation. Even her white face was a dirty grey.

The first thing we did was to prepare her for X-ray and while Brian Coles anaesthetized her, Lesley, his dedicated and sympathetic nurse, brought in the film on which we carefully positioned her, lightly strapping down the wing tips to hold them still. We kept Avis under anaesthetic while Lesley processed and returned the film which revealed a compound fracture at the base of the right humerus near the dislocated and chipped elbow joint.

Once again the fracture was on the right wing. It is an interesting fact that I have found more than twice as many broken or dislocated right wings as left ones. I believe that this is due to the barn owl's low slow flight when it leaves its hunting post beside the road to cross from one verge to the other in search of voles. While crossing the near-side traffic lane it will only rise from three to five feet. It is vulnerable to cars and can easily suffer damage to the right wing. If it reaches the offside traffic lane, it will usually have gained sufficient height to clear a car, although it still may be hit by a higher vehicle. On the interchanges of motorways where there are large grassy areas, the barn owl perches on crash barriers when searching the grass for food, and is unlikely to rise sharply enough from its 30 inch observation post to avoid a vehicle passing close by.

After close study of the X-ray, Brian opened up the muscle surrounding the humerus, and cleaned and inserted the exposed section of the bone, holding it in place and stitching up the surrounding aperture. The full recovery of the dislocation was out of the question at this point, because not only was the elbow chipped and the surrounding tissue badly torn, but the injury was too near the joint to manipulate both dislocation and fracture at the same time.

After some time in the nursing cage, further operations were performed to rectify the drooping wing and the damaged elbow, but it was evident that Avis would never be able to return to her wild and free existence. Only a bird that is completely fit can possibly survive in nature's hostile environment.

When her injuries had healed and she was fit and able to hold her wing normally at rest, moving it sufficiently to give her some lift and balance, Avis was put outside into the aviary until a partner could be found for her. Considering the extent of her injuries, I give Brian Coles great credit for even saving the wing, let alone providing her with the ability to use it, although he himself is never satisfied unless a wild creature can be restored fit and well to its natural life.

In the few weeks before the discovery of Avis, five others were found dead a mile or so away, a few hundred yards north of the Carnforth intersection. No doubt they also had been drawn to the motorway when they had become unable to find voles around their natural and long-established nest site, three or four miles away in a derelict building. Although there was no way of identifying these owls, these repeated accidents may have caused the total loss of that year's young and parents from the derelict building. Two years previously, eight dead barn owls were counted in a space of twelve weeks on a short stretch of the M6 north of Penrith.

If the scale of mortality that occurred on this relatively short length of motorway is repeated elsewhere, and if the many birds I have found either injured or dead in the so-called quiet country lanes of Cumbria are anything to go by, then the barn owls of our countryside, few as they still are, will need all the protection they can get, despite their widespread nesting.

On a happier note, Beauty and Kirk excelled their 1975 performance the following year by laying four eggs. Naturally we wondered whether they would hatch and rear a full clutch with as much success as before. But they did, and four fine, healthy, nearly full-grown birds, Buff, Breeze, Barno and Bud, visited B.B.C. T.V.'s Pebble Mill programme with their parents to show what can be done, and to try to persuade other veterinary surgeons that caring for wildlife is worth while. Shortly afterwards the four youngsters were separated from their parents and two of them, Barno and Bud, were paired off, as before, with two aviary-bred owls kindly supplied to me by Derek Bunn of Lanchashire.

The other two unpaired birds, Buff and Breeze, were carefully established in barn owl territories, where one or the other of a wild pair had been injured and given to me for medical treatment. The least I could do to keep breeding barn owls in their established sites in those two quiet valleys was to provide a young male, Buff, to replace the injured male, Rus, to one barn where only a female remained, and a young female to another area where the breeding female, Titch, had been injured.

The two paired youngsters—two of mine, Barno and Bud, with two of Derek Bunn's, Chip and Chick—settled well in their prepared barns in late 1976. Both pairs laid eggs, one couple in a barn in Yorkshire and the other couple, Bud and Chick, on a bird reserve, and the eggs hatched but the young were eaten by rats so neither pair had a breeding success. In both cases the nest box had been fixed directly to the horizontal tie of the roof truss which made access easy for predators like rats. All future nest boxes were fixed directly to the barn wall. Unfortunately later that summer the breeding female, Chip, at the farm in Yorkshire was found drowned in a cattle trough, a death which is all too common with both barn and tawny owls.

Early in 1977, Avis, had recovered enough for me to introduce her to Rus as a suitable injured male partner. This breeding partnership produced five healthy owlets. At seventy-five days old, looking just like their parents, they were removed to my large aviary and put with the four other youngsters I had bred and reared that summer.

All were ringed by the British Trust for Ornithology and provided with temporary identification by unique arrangements of coloured plastic rings so that when they sorted themselves out in compatible pairs, each couple in one of the many roosting boxes around the walls, I could note their identity without disturbance. Once the owls were firmly paired the plastic rings were removed.

Every evening at dusk I had great entertainment watching their emergence from their various boxes, and I was reminded of badger-watching as they cautiously peered out. After a careful inspection of the aviary the bolder of the pair would take the initiative, even cocking her head to pick up the slightest sound from the camera or photographer. Finding nothing amiss she would step to the entrance, look upwards and finally once more towards the camera inside the hide. Stepping out on the landing board she would plunge downwards and turn to await her mate.

All were settled in selected barns, some in pairs in a barn at Sedbergh and Dent where they produced five and seven young respectively, and some singly, all destined for release into the wild to help build up the numbers of this rare species. And all came from two injured pairs, now living a useful life. Each summer we await with great excitement the phantom flight of young barn owls over fields and fells like their parents before them. Then they become the unforgettable ghosts in the gloaming.

The lack of suitable nesting sites restricts the natural spread of barn owls and I urge all farmers to leave more odd corners of rough land and consciously to make provision for barn owls in their barns as is done in Europe, by leaving holes in the gable ends at high level and by providing nest sites using tea chests or similar sized boxes fixed to the barn walls.

Lastly but not least, we all should think carefully before giving up more of our fast disappearing countryside to roads and development, and we should urge the Department of the Environment to show much more serious concern for our *natural* environment on which wildlife and ultimately man himself depends for existence.

Diurnal Predators of the Sky

The predatory birds of the daylight hours are very conspicuous and give delight to the naturalist as they use the wind and rising air currents to display to the full their skill in flight. The golden eagle and the osprey head the list for size and rarity, but the buzzard and kestrel, thankfully still quite plentiful, give perhaps the most joy to the largest number of people. They are easy to watch and spectacular in flight. Harriers and the peregrine falcon are rare and not often seen. Sparrow hawks, slightly larger than the kestrel and frequently mistaken for it although their flight and hunting habits are different, are often seen in the countryside, streaking low along the hedgerows and over trees in their pursuit of sparrows, starlings and other small birds. One or two owls fly and hunt by day, the largest being the short-eared owl, while the little owl and the ghostly barn owl are usually seen in the light of early evening.

Under the law, neither bird nor its eggs may be touched or taken from the nest. Some may not even be photographed at the nest unless a licence has been issued by the Nature Conservancy Council. Infringement of the Protection of Birds Act carries penalties of fines, imprisonment and confiscation of birds or eggs, depending on the nature of the offence.

The kestrel, which I have reared and successfully returned to the wild, is a most rewarding bird to nurse and release. Years later it can still be seen hunting over fellside and field. Other daytime predators which have passed through my hands include the handsome short-eared owl, and the difficult sparrow hawk. I was given my first kestrel, Cockey, in August 1971. It came from an aviary, and was quite fit, but was unable to catch and kill its own food. Kestrels are birds with a happy disposition and charming movements.

Once Cockey had become at home in my aviary, hunting lessons started. On the first day, two live mice were introduced in an open box put on its side on the floor. Cocking her head from side to side as she heard the movement of the mice, she flew down, and waddled along in penguin fashion. She gave an occasional jab with one foot and peered inside to see whether the mice were there. As nothing emerged, she returned to her perch but kept such an alert gaze on the box that when a mouse showed itself at the open end, she pounced straight onto it, gripping it in her talons. But when it squeaked she dropped it and flew back to her perch. She continued to watch with sharp forward and backward jerks of the head as the mouse scampered about on the grassy floor. Finally she swooped down, grabbed it in her claws, rose up to her branch and ate it. Several minutes later she caught and killed the second mouse in the same way, but this time she waddled round the aviary, carrying it in her beak, and hid it in a corner.

Cockey responded quickly to her few days' training and within three weeks we opened the aviary door. Out she flew with rapid wing beats and landed on a nearby ash tree, where she rested and took stock of her surroundings. Her next move took her low over a stubble field, where two crows and a magpie mobbed her with such persistence that they brought her to the ground uttering a distressed call. I gave chase and drove off the attackers. None the worse, my kestrel flew up and into a tall hawthorn hedge where she remained until dusk.

Two days later I had the thrill of watching her flying strongly over the fields and after seven days she was hovering head into the wind, her tail and wing feathers adjusting to the change of air pressure, while she scanned the grass below for voles, mice and even beetles.

Gradually her territory enlarged as she hunted far and wide; the last positive sighting occurred six weeks after her release. I recognized her by a plumage mark, hovering over the motorway embankment a few miles away, hunting for bank-voles (*Clethrionomys glareolus*).

Cockey was a relatively easy visitor, being uninjured and healthy and in need of only training to catch live food. The other kestrels which came from my veterinary surgeon and the local R.S.P.C.A. Inspector were injured, deformed and very crippled.

Two such youngsters, Tee-Vee and Jess, were rescued from television aerials. They had been found dangling upside down having become entangled in the metal by strings around their legs. One even had a broken leg as a result of this experience. Another youngster, Ricky, was picked up among houses, completely deformed by rickets. Its legs were twisted up to its breast and it was unable to stand or feed. Tailless, kept in captivity and incorrectly fed at the critical growing stage, it had lost, by breakage, most of its primary and tail feathers. Its flying ability would be impaired until after the moult in the autumn of the following year. All these birds had been stolen illegally from their nests by youths, who had tried to rear them and become amateur 'falconers' without knowing anything about their requirements or behaviour.

The influence of the film *Kes* was brought home to me when four youths, who had discovered where the injured kestrels were being treated, called to request the return of 'their' birds. They stated that they had taken the nestlings in imitation of Casper in the film, and did not realize that their actions were illegal. On the two occasions when the B.B.C. showed this film, I requested the Royal Society for the Protection of Birds to make representations, and a well-worded statement was made at the end of each performance, reminding viewers that what Casper had done in the film was illegal.

On an earlier occasion I had been interviewed on the B.B.C. television programme 'Pebble Mill at One', and in May 1976 they co-operated splendidly once more. I took Jess, one of my most endearing kestrels, and she behaved magnificently. The feature, which was televised in the grounds of Pebble Mill, was introduced by David Seymour who held the kestrel on his hand while he explained the consequences of stealing young kestrels. I then took over the hawk, and with the aid of slides of injured kestrels, showed how these stolen birds are often later found with broken legs. This is usually due to amateur 'falconers' fitting strings as jesses. They then become entangled in television aerials or trees when the kestrels escape.

A brisk breeze was blowing, which the bird enjoyed immensely, and she showed herself off before the television cameras to everyone's delight. The whole programme was most successful in emphasizing the message that kestrels should not be taken by amateurs to train as falcons, and that their rightful place is flying free in the wild for all to enjoy.

My spate of injured kestrels continued, and three more adult females, Screamer, Scholar and Lady, entered my aviary where they were prepared for life in the wild. One boy who tired of trying to train Screamer, but who did not wish to harm her, sensibly handed her in to Tony Crittenden of the R.S.P.C.A., who passed her on to me. She would flap her wings and scream for food when she saw anyone approach, and this made her a difficult bird to return to the wild. Lady had been kept tethered by a lady as a pet, and Scholar was found with a strained wing near a school. Although it is not easy, with care and patience such birds can have their ability to kill their own food developed, and can be safely and successfully sent back to the wild.

All birds are examined as soon as they arrive and if injured an X-ray is taken by my helpful veterinary surgeon, Brian Coles. Tee-Vee, although not physically injured, had hung upside down for over twenty-four hours on an aerial, and when first put in his treatment cage, he turned his head over completely to view the outside world. His tender age was revealed when he backed to the edge of the box to eject his excreta, in the manner of all young birds of prey in the nest when they are nearly ready to fly.

On occasions this bird became very frustrated and, after scuffing furiously in the sawdust of the nursing cage, and shredding up paper, resorted to violent wing-flapping and screaming. When he became stronger and no longer had an upside down view of the world, he was transferred to the aviary where he soon settled down, and celebrated the transfer with a bath, splashing the water all over the place, popping in and out several times until satisfied.

Mouse-hunting was in full swing when Screamer arrived. She was put straight into the aviary with Tee-Vee, and although he was a very young bird, he held his own, with much sparring, showing the newcomer that this was his aviary and that he was the boss. They quickly became close friends, roosting tightly together every night. Though the mature female was very tame and begged for food to be given to her by hand, I completely ignored her fluttering wings and screaming, and she was left to pick up her food from the aviary floor or go without. The active youngster alongside provided competition and she soon realized that if she did not quickly snatch her prey from the floor and eat it, Tee-Vee certainly would. Progress was good and as this adult female was never hand-fed by me, she soon abandoned her fluttering and shrieking, and lived a contented existence with the young male.

Ricky, doubled up with rickets, posed a real problem too, for her legs were twisted up around her breast and neck. The young bird had become deformed while in the care of youths who obviously knew nothing of her feeding requirements and had callously cast her out into the streets to die. By good fortune she had been picked up by a sympathetic person and brought to me.

Many who saw this pathetic young bird suggested it would be more humane to put her down, as there was no chance of correcting such a serious deformity. Such words, and my anger against those who had brought her to this state, provided me with the challenge, and after consultation with my vet, I kept her in the nursing cage and hand fed her every few hours with pieces of mouse and day-old chicks, supplemented with vitamins and minerals. This was a very tedious business, because, being unable to stand, she fouled her feathers when she excreted, and so had to be washed every time to prevent the droppings becoming encrusted on her plumage.

For five weeks Ricky was under intensive care. When I had to be away from home a friend of mine, Jean Bryne, a keen admirer of all birds of prey, took the kestrel to her home and gave the bird the greatest possible care and attention. The nursing cage was kept on the kitchen table, making close observation easy, and as the bird became stronger she was allowed out in the evening into the room to spread her wings for exercise.

Gradually her twisted legs grew stronger, and there was great joy when she was at last able to stand on a log in her cage, a real character with bossy behaviour and cheeky ways.

Towards evening she would poke her head through the large mesh of the cage and peer around in the hope that someone would open the door. At this time she was often visited by one of the three family cats, who jumped onto the table and sat in front of the cage as if to see what all the fuss was about. The cat never showed any inclination to touch the bird. His interest was in the dead day-old chicks used for feeding, which he drew out with his paw through the bars and then ate. It was not until Jean came into the kitchen one day and found the cat with his foreleg fully extended through the bars, dragging the chicks towards the front, that she realized why the kestrel seemed to be consuming so many chicks. Meanwhile the kestrel looked on from her perch on the log cocking her head from side to side. Nothing would dissuade the cat from stealing the chicks, so fine wire-netting was fixed to the cage front. This rather spoiled the pleasure of the kestrel, who enjoyed poking her head through the bars to look into the room.

Releasing Ricky in the kitchen each evening not only provided her with the opportunity of flying around and exploring, but gave her excellent facilities for using her feet and claws, landing on, and clinging to, the curtain rail, pictures and chairbacks. In this way she developed her latent muscles. As her legs and claws became stronger she spent less time sitting like a feathered puff-ball roosting on her log, and usually stood in the natural manner, even developing sufficient strength to roost on one leg with the other foot tucked up into her breast feathers.

Using her ciné camera Jean took some excellent film of the kestrel playing with objects and showing off to the onlooker with all the intelligence of a primate. The kestrel would perch on various objects on the sideboard top and look at her reflection in the shiny surface, twisting her head right over and jerking it from side to side. Jumping down onto the top, she would flatten herself on her breast with wings and tail outspread, and shuffle furiously with her legs, as though having a really vigorous bath. She would complete this behaviour by sitting on a vase and preening. Obviously she mistook the shiny top for water.

Her claws on one foot became quite efficient at gripping, but two of the toes on the other foot never straightened. She could now stand on her prey and grip, and was able to tear off pieces with her beak, but further improvement was imperative if she was to grip, kill and eat small mammals in the wild.

Playing with a chromium nut, part of Jean's photographic equipment, did much to help develop her claws and became a fascinating game. When the nut was dropped accidentally and went spinning away across the floor, it was rapidly followed by the kestrel. She flew down, waddled up to it, and stood peering down, jerking her head in characteristic kestrel manner. Then as if playing with a mouse, she ran round it, occasionally jabbing it with one foot and sending it sliding across the floor. Chasing after it, she pounced and grabbed it, gripping it tightly in her claws, then hopped away on one foot while holding on to the shining nut triumphantly with the other. She would then deliberately drop it again, and with pounces and jerks of the foot, play football round the floor, eventually picking it up in her beak and carrying it off to a shelf.

Sometimes she just played with the pattern on the floor and many times would collapse on its shiny surface, shuffling vigorously with her legs and propelling herself along. On one occasion she flew through into the back kitchen and landed on the formica-topped table, which had been set with knives and forks. She toddled round looking for mischief and had soon sent a knife spinning. This aroused her interest and, peering down in her attractive way, she kicked out at it with her foot, sending it skimming across the table. She followed rapidly, and pounced when it was precariously balanced over the edge of the table. As it dropped to the floor she swooped after it and continued to 'kill' it by jabbing and pouncing. This kestrel play was not only highly entertaining to watch, and invaluable filmed evidence to have of these birds' ability to play, but was, I am convinced, the main reason for the almost complete recovery of that particular bird.

Once she was transferred to the aviary, which she shared with Tailless, she rapidly discovered her normal predatory instincts. The first thing she did was to have a real drenching bath in the tin of water on the floor, instead of the dry simulated baths she had enjoyed on the sideboard top and floor. Mouse training started and both she and Tailless progressed well.

Ricky, despite her two twisted claws, became an efficient killer of small rodents. When perched, her claws were the only reminder of that pathetic bird of prey which I had been advised to destroy.

It was now too late in the year for release, and in any case the tailless kestrel had to grow a new tail. So both were kept over the winter. They were transferred to the large aviary between the cottage and the oakwoods, and when release was due they were ringed by a member of the British Trust for Ornithology. I was particularly intrigued to observe that now, when presented with live mice, they had become selective in the choice of the colour of their home-bred food, rejecting both albino and black mice, and would only kill and eat the brown and dark grey ones. In the wild, the small mammals on which kestrels feed are brown field-mice and short-tailed voles, and dark grey shrews. Was their selection coincidental or was it instinctive? Had they been the only two birds of prey exhibiting this interesting behaviour I would have said it was coincidental, but as three other kestrels and a buzzard, reared separately, displayed the same peculiarity, I can say with some certainty that it must have been instinctive.

In early July several fine days were forecast, and as this was weather best suited for their release I gave the two kestrels the morning in which to feed in the aviary, and then prepared to set them free. This was the moment for which I had been waiting all these months. It was calm and sunny, with a feeling of spring in the air. I caught and examined my once-crippled kestrel, Ricky, put any ruffled feather back neatly into place and held her aloft, head into the wind, and let her legs slip from between my fingers. She rose swiftly on fast-beating wings as I bade her good hunting. Up she went over the tops of the trees and came to rest not very far away. Quickly collecting the handsome grey and rufous male, Tailless, who now had a long and perfect tail, I let him take off into the wind, hoping he would find his mate.

A shrill call came from the trees as they made contact, and on powerful wings they flew across the open ground, rising up high above the valley on a thermal. Each soared motionless like a buzzard, rising higher and higher, occasionally flicking a tail and wing as though to let out every feather in such free and far-reaching flight. Occasionally they flapped their wings and chased each other, enjoying the up-currents to the full, growing smaller and smaller as they rose into the vast wide space. After climbing about a thousand feet on the air-current, the female dipped a wing, tipped over to one side and streaked away out of sight down wind, followed by her mate.

It was sheer joy and delight, after so many months of care and training, to be rewarded by such splendour of flight. Who could condemn such masters of the air to captivity, and to man's command, or allow the cruelty they had once suffered? These kestrels, recognizable through binoculars by the rings on their legs, are still hovering over field and fell after six years and continuing to rear their young in the woods.

In July 1974 Jess was found hanging from a television aerial, with her two feet tied together by a crudely made leather thong. The R.S.P.C.A. Inspector who carried out the rescue considered this to be the work of an amateur 'falconer'. All except one of my kestrels have been the victims of such illegal pursuits, but in this case the poor bird also had a broken leg. She was only a few weeks old, and was treated by Brian Coles who X-rayed and pinned the leg and gave her to me for care and nursing.

I kept her in the nursing cage until, after three weeks, the pin was removed. She could only use one leg and, depending as she did on the grip of both feet for survival, she caused concern. But after she had been transferred to the aviary her condition improved enormously. Not only did she do much bathing and preening, but she had ample exercise for her injured leg as she flew from branch to branch, gripping with her claws. She soon learnt to stand on her food with both feet and to tear off pieces of meat with her beak.

I wondered how she would kill when she was first given live mice. She was quick to catch and hold and, in her excitement it seemed, she forgot her bad leg, gripping and standing on both equally well while killing. She became such an avid hunter that by mid-September she was even chasing and catching the blue tits which flew through the mesh in the aviary.

The next few days were forecast fine and sunny, and as she

too was selecting her mice for food, at mid-day I rolled back the wire aviary roof and she flew to freedom. Her first resting place was the top of a larch tree. During the first few critical days I kept a look out for her, and on the fifth day saw her standing up for herself against two magpies. She took no notice and flew off. I saw her twice later on, using the wind, hovering over the verges on the track beside the cottage, but I was glad when she moved over to the rough fellside, away from the woodland which gives cover to the tormenting crows, magpies, jackdaws and jays.

Short-eared owls, slightly smaller than the tawny owl, are hunters by day, quartering the rough open marshes, estuaries and moorland for voles. Their flight is often low and rolling, with deep slow beats of the wings followed by frequent glides. These reveal their pale tawny, brown and cream colouring, with dark carpal patches and light streaks on the upper surface of the wing which makes them resemble large fritillary butterflies. They have a rather 'fierce' expression, with their golden eyes and 'scowling' face, like the little owl. The short-eared owl gets its name from the small tufts of feathers above the eyes. As with other owls, their ears are at the side of the head, behind the facial disc, which at night stands forward (especially in the tawny owl) to reveal dark crescent-shaped apertures, through which the owl picks up every minute sound. The short-eared owl nests on the ground in long grass or rushes, and as the 'ear' tufts are erect when relaxed and down when alarmed, I am convinced their purpose is camouflage, to break up the otherwise round full-moon face.

In my aviary, one long-eared owl often roosted during the daytime in a tall, slim cigar-shaped position with eyes closed and 'ear' tufts erect. However slowly and carefully I approached it would gradually sink down, retracting the tufts, and with open eyes its face became round and menacing. Long-eared owls being entirely nocturnal are seldom seen, because their daytime roosting position, usually against the trunk of a conifer, provides most effective camouflage.

My short-eared owl was picked up in Kent as an immature bird, and cared for by David Pedge of Gillingham, who reared it successfully on day-old chicks and dead mice, bred for the purpose. His aim was to return it to the wild, and he offered the bird to the Hawk Trust for breeding. The Trust, knowing of my success at returning birds of prey to their natural environment, and seeing that it was a fully-winged healthy bird, asked me if I could help.

The owl, carefully packed in a sturdy box specially constructed for the purpose, was dispatched by Red Star Freight from Euston Station, and collected by me in Liverpool less than three hours later. In next to no time this magnificent bird was unpacked and stretching its wings in a large aviary.

Only a day after its arrival it was completely at home in the aviary, which it shared with a kestrel. Live mouse training was started at once. It had already been fed on dead mice, and knew immediately how to react to the mice provided. With its powerful claws it soon discovered that one quick grip around the small animal was sufficient to kill it. As with all my birds of prey, it was ringed before its release, and taken onto the moors, the natural habitat of a short-eared owl in the summer.

John Webster, my farmer friend, was delighted to have such a bird on his upland farm, as he had seen the occasional one hunting for voles among the tussocky mountain grass. The day chosen for its release was sunny with a light breeze. Birds such as the short-eared owl have very savage claws, and it used them to the full when we tried to take it out of the carrying box, but once it was in the hand, though ready to be away, it remained quite placid. It surveyed the vast miles of open moorland and valleys while I held it by the legs on top of the high stone wall. For several minutes this handsome fierce-eyed bird scanned the countryside, then with a heavy beat of its long wings it flew low across the rough moorland of marsh and cotton grass, to rise up and over the far drystone wall, and away to the hills and freedom. I wished it well in the vast wilderness, and hoped that it would soon find a partner, before it migrated to the estuaries for winter.

Isabel Paton of North Yorkshire brought me my first little owl, Dot, to prepare for a life in the wild. Dot had been reared from a fledgling and had grown into a typically active and bright-eyed adult. Later I had the pleasurable experience of rearing Denis, a fledgling who soon developed bushy eyebrows and piercing eyes even before he had lost his youthful down.

Most people instinctively like little owls as they are miniatures, the size of a song thrush, and their gaze is so intense. One interesting characteristic is the white V on the back of the head which exactly matches the white V of the eyebrows. In the distance it is not possible to tell which way the bird is looking and this protects the owl from predators attacking from behind.

When its curiosity is aroused the little owl bobs up and down on its surprisingly long legs. As they are shy birds this is usually followed by a quick darting flight into a dark hole. If caught they will lie quite still on their backs in the hand and can be examined or ringed without any fuss. During the mating season a pair makes most entertaining calls, the male giving a rising musical hoot and the female answering with a low and seemingly uninterested grunt.

Earthworms and insects form the main diet with occasional small rodents, so both Dot and Denis had to be given the opportunity to catch such food in their large grass-floored aviary. As soon as they could manage this efficiently they were released into farmland with old trees forming suitable little owl territory. Dot was the forerunner of several other interesting and attractive little owls.

One of the most spectacular diurnal predators of the sky is the sparrow hawk. But it is extremely difficult to care for in captivity, as I experienced when nursing a female called Spag, in 1971, and later, in 1975, another female named Sabre.

The adult female, Spag, was collected from South Wales, having developed a tumour on the upper joint of her left wing. An operation was performed to remove the growth, and she was given to me for post-operative care. At that time I had not begun using my nursing cage, so to prevent excess wing movement she was tethered by jesses to a block in the same aviary as my first tawny owl. This allowed sufficient movement without strain.

Considerable improvement followed the operation, and the stiffness of the joint gradually eased with the removal of the stitches and gentle exercise. Unfortunately I had to be away from home for a while and by the time I returned, the bird, now much stronger, had gone to join several other birds of prey in the large aviary of a friend. Although she lived amicably with the tawny owls and kestrels, she had not bargained for the chivvying she received from an old crow, which I had not realized would be one of her inmates. She feared him from the start and when he attacked her she rolled over on her back striking out with her legs in self-defence. She had no corner into which to retreat, and the crow's attentions proved too much for her. Highly strung and of a nervous temperament she started having fits. Sparrow hawks are susceptible to fits when under stress, and as her keeper had no alternative accommodation, she died before my vet could do anything to save her.

Sabre, although badly damaged, was more fortunate. She was a magnificent bird, with a brown-grey back and wings, striped tail and rufous and cream horizontally-striped breast. Like Spag, she had piercing yellow eyes, hooked beak and powerful claws.

As she flew across a valley in Wales in pursuit of her prey, a shot rang out and she fell crippled to the woodland floor. Fortunately she was spotted by a young boy on holiday, who had compassion for helpless creatures and went to her rescue. As the lad crept closer to the bird it fluttered along the ground trying to avoid capture, and let out a series of shrieks as he gently put his hands around her. She went over on her back striking out with her feet and pecking with her powerful hooked beak. He closed the wings to the bird's side and picked her up carefully, put her in a box and took her home. On the next day he took her to his veterinary surgeon to see what damage had been done. By an odd coincidence this boy lived not many miles from my home, and his vet was also my excellent vet, so the bird was in good hands.

That Monday evening I happened to take my beagle along to see Brian Coles, and as I entered the surgery he said he had received something that morning which, he was sure, would be of interest to me. He went behind the scenes and returned with this handsome female sparrow hawk. The shot had gone through the right wing fracturing the ulna and metacarpal bones. As the ulna was virtually splinted by the parallel radius bone, it was decided not to pin, but to keep the bird in close confinement, allowing no excessive movement of the wings, but just sufficient for it to preen and prevent the muscles from wasting.

Sparrow hawks are very temperamental birds in captivity, and for two days this one showed no signs of feeding on the various natural dead food, such as sparrows or mice, I provided for her. On the third day two small boys appeared on the doorstep with a pathetic little bluetit, from which one wing had been torn by a cat. Obviously it was in a very shocked state and would never be able to fly. After close examination I thought it would be more humane to destroy it than to try to save it. So I put it down and gave it, while still very fresh and warm, to the sparrow hawk to see if really fresh food would tempt her. That little bluetit was a godsend. I am convinced it saved the life of the rare predator, for not only did Sabre eat the bluetit, she continued straight on to the dead sparrows, which showed she must have been extremely hungry.

After a couple of week's rest in the nursing cage, it was decided to strap the badly drooping wing lightly. A fortnight later the strapping was removed and the fracture X-rayed. The breaks were not completely healed, so Sabre was returned to her cage for a further ten days, without strapping, by which time she was ready to be transferred to the large aviary. I took the opportunity to ring her as I hoped eventually to return her to a life of freedom.

Sparrow hawks do not adapt readily to aviary conditions, and after fluttering around for some time she sat on a branch for the rest of the day. Successful flying would not be possible until the muscles were completely restored. She never fully accepted the netting, and although she had her own darkened corner, at dusk she struggled to get out and spend the night sheltering in the large nearby hedge. Since she had not eaten all day, she was returned to the familiar nursing cage, and eventually took her food that evening. Next day she was put out for exercise, but she would not eat, so she was returned again to her cage at dusk.

After a couple of weeks her wing was examined again under X-ray. This showed that the fractures had now healed; but she had lost about ten degrees of movement in that wing, which gave Brian Coles some concern for her future in the wild. At the beginning of May she was transferred to the large aviary near the oak woods, and she looked superb in the sun, surrounded by her natural woodland setting of spring green and golden oak trees. Hordes of tits, chaffinches and other small birds soon discovered her, and came and sat on the hazel bushes beside the aviary, scolding and shouting abuse. On a branch above, a mistle-thrush stood uttering her harsh churring chatter of disgust at this predator. As her scolding had little effect, she passed backwards and forwards over the top of the aviary, dive bombing to within a few inches of the roof netting. Sabre watched and ducked every time she came near her head.

As I had to go to the New Forest for three weeks, to do some work on the wildlife there, a colleague, Tony Warburton, very experienced in the idiosyncrasies of birds of prey, came and took her into his care at his home near the Cumbrian coast. He, like myself, was thrilled and delighted to have her, and gladly accepted the challenge of restoring her to the wild.

Until Sabre had accepted her changed environment and was feeding again, having recognized Tony as her friend, she was kept in a small area, more particularly as she was moulting. By the time June arrived, Sabre looked fit and well and was then transferred to a vast aviary with extensive views across field and fellside, woodland and hedgerows, where the skylark and pipit, starling and chaffinch feed, and the barn owl, on large laboured wings, hunts at dusk. She accepted this aviary, with its more spacious surroundings, without demur. She shared it with an elderly tawny owl, who showed little concern for her presence.

Sabre's wings rapidly became stronger, and she manoeuvred and twisted about, hanging upside down on the netting roof. This showed that she now had the necessary dexterity to dart and turn when she chased small birds in the wild for food. Tony gave me a report of Sabre's excellent progress, and asked me what should be the next move. As the meadows around his aviary had just been cut, and the weather was hot and dry at the peak of summer, I suggested that he might try out Sabre's wings in the open, unhampered by the netting of the aviary.

To prevent her from flying away before we were sure she was completely recovered, jesses were fixed to her legs and a long thin creance tied to them. This was laid out loosely over the field, giving plenty of flight room for testing her wings. Daily exercise was taken in this manner, and Sabre gave Tony much delight and satisfaction when she stretched her wings at full spread, improving every day in her strength and movement.

On a glorious Sunday afternoon I went over to witness Sabre in flight to decide whether the time had come for release. She stood on Tony's hand as he carried her from the aviary to the meadows, and she proudly scanned the wide open countryside with her fierce yellow eyes. The creance was spread out across the field to reduce drag, and when all was ready the hawk took off low across the grass on fast wing beat, rising as though making for a high hedge, but checked when all the slack in the creance had been taken up. On a second flight she performed even better, her wings beating hard into the wind. Landing some distance away, she stood in the short grass looking around while a meadow pipit dived and mobbed her.

The crucial decision had now to be made before she became over-tired. With little hesitation I gave the long-awaited words: 'Off with the jesses and let her go free.' At three o'clock on that perfect Sunday afternoon we stood back as the jesses were slipped. Away she streaked, low across the field on rapid wings, with long grey tail and bright yellow legs hanging slightly down. To our horror she seemed to be heading straight for some sheep netting at the edge of the field, and both Tony and I held our breath, knowing only too well what would happen if she flew into it. But with the strength and speed of a powerful wild sparrow hawk, though only just in time, she rose steeply and landed twenty feet up in a hawthorn hedge.

I watched her with a sigh of relief and a feeling of joy and exhilaration for she had won back her wings and was once more wild and free. We crept closer, expecting her to be breathing heavily after such exertion. But she stood there in the branches, unconcerned, scanning her wild environment before taking off once more. This time she rose up out of the branches, flew over the top of the hedge and away across a kale field, coming to rest in an ash tree at the far side. We bade this fine raptor farewell and returned to the house, talking over what we had witnessed. We expressed our joy at the recovery Sabre had made, first at the hands of the boy who picked her up, then with the expert care and patience of Brian Coles, and finally the careful after-treatment and nursing she had received in captivity.

But more thrilling news was yet to come when seven weeks later Tony sent me this message. 'At dusk on 15 September I was watching the wild owlets from the field where Sabre flew when we released her. I was sitting in the hedge bottom, next to a small dead hawthorn tree. Suddenly I became aware of a large bird hurtling straight towards me a few feet from the ground. It was head on but my impression was of a very deep chested, powerful bird. It came right up to my tree, swooped up and perched ten feet from where I was sitting — and there was Sabre, perfect, ring and all! She was in beautiful condition, flying like an arrow, and obviously in blooming health. After sitting there for thirty seconds or so she suddenly became aware of me and was gone in a flash. What a thrill! I cannot tell you of my feelings at that moment, when I saw the familiar ring on this magnificent bird, but I know you will both share my joy that a once helpless cripple had made such a complete recovery. What a reward for all your efforts and patience, and what a reward for the skills of your marvellous vet!' I was intensely moved when I read this letter. Only those who know and have cared for such fine creatures can share our feelings. Three years later she is still seen hunting the fields and hedgerows.

For many years I have watched, with tremendous admiration, the buzzards gliding round in circles above the cottage on broad motionless wings. I wanted to see this noble bird close at hand, to study its form and build, and to discover why it had such ability and grace.

I knew that the buzzard, one of our largest breeding birds, was often illegally shot by gamekeepers, but I had never heard of anyone attempting to save an injured bird and put it back on the wing. I had always longed to do this, but none had ever come my way. Suddenly, out of the blue, one September morning, Tony Crittenden of the R.S.P.C.A. rang me to say that he and a colleague were going to collect a magnificent bird (species not stated) which he felt I would like, hoping that I could accommodate and train it to return to its natural environment. I groaned as my accommodation was full. But when they told me the bird was a buzzard, I immediately agreed to take it. I just hoped that only training and not much nursing would be needed.

The buzzard had been purchased and kept in close captivity by a man who was also illegally keeping a barn owl and a kestrel, though these were well fed and healthy. They were to be collected with a view to release.

On 10 September the buzzard arrived in a wicker basket, which proved a most unfortunate choice of container as the head of the bird had been severely damaged on the sharp ends of the cane on the inside of the lid. Birds should always be carried in smooth containers such as a cardboard box, particularly the R.S.P.C.A. purpose-made cardboard container, which is most suitable and readily available.

Inside the thirty-foot-long aviary the jesses were removed from the buzzard's legs, the damaged head was dusted with antibiotic powder and the bird released. At dusk the head treatment was repeated and a couple of dead day-old chicks put out, one of which she took immediately. This showed that she had recovered her composure and was feeling better than she looked. I had no idea of the sex of the buzzard, but somehow its behaviour always made me think the bird was female.

Brian called next day to check the head damage, and was appalled at her injury. The treatment was good, and we continued it night and morning, until the raw area dried and healed. At this stage baldness seemed inevitable, but eventually, to my relief, a minute stubble of feathers began to show and I knew then that full recovery was possible.

Flying freely from one end of the aviary to the other, Buzz settled down well and obviously enjoyed herself. A favourite perch was a padded post on which she slept like a headless puff-ball, with her head tucked between her wings. As she was making such good progress it was time to wean her from the diet of chicks to natural food like mice, voles, sparrows and rabbits. But for nine months she had been fed entirely on chicks, and she would take nothing else. Thinking that she was addicted to the bright yellow of the chicks, I dyed them dark brown, but she was not to be fooled, and ate them as usual. The first break came when I put down a live mouse on the aviary floor and she took an interest in it.

The extensive aviary was originally a raspberry cage, but few canes were left intact, and the ground was now covered with chick weed, mint and other vegetation, which provided good cover for a mouse and gave Buzz a natural background in which to seek her prey.

Fortunately she had not yet completed her annual moult, so her head feathers grew well and several tail and flight feathers were shed and regrown. The feather pattern across her large breast resembled a mayoral chain, as in general her breast was dark mottled plumage, but the arc of light feathers curved downwards from the base of one wing across the breast to the other. This made her all the more intriguing at night as she slept on her post, her head buried out of sight in her fluffy feathers.

Brian, who is also a keen photographer, showed a great interest in her, and naturally was anxious to take some photographs. One lunch-time in October he came round, and as no bird likes being gripped round the legs by hand, I put on jesses and took her through the hedge, into the open field. It was a dull day, but a strong wind was blowing and as this was her first time out I did not know how she would react. Standing into the wind with wings outstretched, her weight being taken on the strong breeze, she felt as light as the proverbial feather. She gazed around and provided a very photogenic subject. As the wind rose and fell she altered the span of her wings and spread of her tail to hold herself lightly on my hand, and at her full wing-span of almost five feet she resembled a large model aircraft about to take off into the gale.

I was impressed by her gentleness and her ready acceptance of training, so unlike kestrels who shout their defiance and hatred of handling. When I held Buzz on my hand she occasionally put her head down in front of me and tenderly preened the front of my jumper in the same gentle manner as one of my early tawny owls, who used to croon to me as he combed my hair with his foot. Or she would press her soft breast against mine, peering at me with her golden eyes as she chirped softly to me in her inimitable way, her savage-looking hooked beak only inches from my face. Often I went into the aviary to see her, and as I approached, quietly talking to her, she would stir herself, stretching her wings upwards in a heraldic position, and chirping her reply to show her pleasure at my company. Fortunately for her future safety she disliked the approach of strangers to her aviary, and flushed wildly around the netting in her endeavour to get as far away as possible.

Food training went well and Buzz completely abandoned her diet of chicks, preferring a diet of live mice and rabbits. Whenever I emerged from the mouse-house, she craned her head and neck in my direction in anticipation of a good meal, and anxiously awaited my arrival with a live mouse. Buzzards are comparatively lazy hunters, and she would sit for some time watching mouse movements among the vegetation on the aviary floor, then turn away and look skywards for a second or two before looking down again to see where the mouse had gone. When the mouse, quite unconcerned, settled down to feed, Buzz would waddle down a sloping branch and across the ground to within a foot of the busy little creature. After scanning her surroundings the bird would shoot out a long powerful leg, grab the mouse in her claws and grip it tightly for several seconds until it was dead, then fly up to her eating post and swallow it in a moment.

On numerous occasions she was visited by a female kestrel, who regularly perched on the end twig of the ash tree above the aviary, looking down and shouting fiercely at the large predator within. After several minutes the kestrel would drop to within six feet of the netting over the aviary roof and hover there squawking continuously until she rose up and stood once more on the tip of her twig. She was for all the world like a spider dropping on an invisible web, pulling up suddenly at the allotted six feet from the roof, where she hung suspended for many moments.

The time came to release Buzz in the wild natural habitat of oak woods and fells, so she was transported to her Lakeland home in a smooth wooden box, with the inside top padded with

Jess, one of my most endearing kestrels

Ricky in flight

Buzz shortly after her arrival

Just before her release

Buzz had a wing span of
almost five feet

expanded polystyrene to prevent any injury to her head if she jumped up and down. Care was taken to avoid any edges on which she could catch and damage her plumage and within three hours she was moved from one aviary to another.

The oak wood's aviary, which was smaller than the thirty foot flight she came from, made her look enormous and more like a golden eagle than a buzzard. Even with all the care taken, the move was not without its setbacks. Due to stress, Buzz went off her food and this affected her internal condition. A little aureomycin powder on food would have put her right, but this was out of the question as she had no interest in eating. Administering a drug by injection was the only way, and in capturing her in the smaller aviary I was disappointed to see her break a primary feather, as I like all my birds to be perfect on release. Although her droppings appeared better next day, she now suffered the effects of the antibiotic injection. It was three days before she had completely recovered and was once again watching with interest all movements inside and outside her aviary. When four buzzards glided mewing overhead, she craned her neck to look up, turning her head completely upwards to watch them, until they passed out of view. No doubt as soon as she was hatched she recognized the calls of her parents circling above or calling to each other, and although she was stolen from the nest when young, and had spent her life as a captive creature, she must still have remembered these sounds of her infancy.

The appointed day for her release arrived, a glorious clear and sunny day with a moderate wind. The autumn fells stood out under an intense blue sky. Normally I would never release a bird as late in the season as early November, but to keep Buzz through the winter would have caused her more stress since she was by now totally dependent on live food and thus very ready to be free. Diurnal birds of prey have more difficulties after release than nocturnal raptors, for not only are they dependent on small mammals, which are basically nocturnal, for the main part of their diet, but they have not the peace of the night, away from human disturbance, in which to seek out and catch their prey. Also, unlike the birds of the night, who have very little opposition from other competitors for the same food, the diurnal birds have much competition and harassment from countless jackdaws, magpies, crows and the other members of the *corvidae* species.

In order to allow sufficient time for a good meal before her departure from the aviary, mid-day was chosen as the time of release. A bird is unlikely to find food the first day out in a strange world, so a good feed is desirable before leaving. One o'clock was the very latest time for release in these short winter days, so a watch was kept all morning to see if and when she ate.

By noon she had occasionally cocked her head in the direction of mice on the aviary floor, but had made no serious move to capture them. I became uneasy at her reluctance to eat, and was beginning to wonder what we could do if she did not. Suddenly she dropped from her perch onto the floor and I held my breath lest some slight sound should cause her to fly up again, and put her off feeding for some hours. She cocked her head and waddled up to a mouse and grabbed it with her powerful talons. With a lift of her wings she rose to her eating perch and stood there for many seconds looking down at her prey. My relief was great as she tore off large pieces, swallowing them in gulps. She must have been hungry, to eat so greedily. She cleaned each claw in turn, then wiped her beak on her perch, first one side and then on the other as though stropping a knife. She looked pleased with her morsel, small though it was. I told myself that I would be delighted if she had just one more before she departed, knowing that she seldom ate more than two at a time. It was as though she read my thoughts, for she went straight down to the floor again, immediately hopped a few feet and clutched a second mouse in her claws. She stood there for a few seconds, first glancing down at her mouse, then casually around her until she had killed it. Much more daintily than before she tore off small pieces, finally swallowing the remains.

I knew now that she had eaten her fill, so I collected up her jesses and slipped them on her legs. This enabled me to walk her around the garden so that she could scan the world outside her aviary. She was delighted to feel the wind under her wings and she spread herself out as the air caressed her feathers.

Occasionally she stood close, her body resting against me while she made her gentle contact chirps, so unexpected from such a large majestic creature. Many times with impatience she tugged at the bonds which held her legs, and I tried to assure her that in only another minute or two she would be unshackled and free to fly where she pleased.

I wanted her to go without flurry or fluster; then making my last contact with her, I removed her jesses and said, 'The world is now yours, away to the woods and the fells'. She looked round for a second, then on those broad brown wings with striking white underparts, she lifted her massive form and in no time at all was through the trees, up over the woods and away.

It was, at that moment, as though my soul departed with her. Although many of my birds have thus flown to freedom, I suddenly felt stunned and alone. I knew the purpose of having her was to prepare her as best I possibly could for that very moment, but somehow her departure stabbed me to the heart. I have had many, many wild creatures to care for, and I have grown fond of some of them. Although the time I had Buzz was shorter than with some, a closer rapport had developed between us than with any previous creature except, perhaps, my first badger. I think it was her size and power combined with her incredible gentleness which had endeared her to me, and I knew I would miss her very much.

The days and nights which follow a release are haunted by concern for my creatures, and I spend much time watching from window and garden, always hoping for that reassuring glimpse. On rough wet nights I reach the depths of despair and wonder how they can be managing, and when the day dawns bright and sunny I scan the skies for signs of their flight. At least four fine days immediately after release could make the difference between success and failure. In the case of Buzz, who flew to freedom in November, this was difficult to arrange. The third day brought torrential rain, some snow and sleet, and high winds, and although I knew she was well fed and trained to feed naturally, my heart sank. I toured the area by car scanning the sky with my binoculars in search of her, not wishing to visit her possible territory on foot in case she might, at that moment, be in the act of catching her prey and would be disturbed.

The fourth day arrived bright, clear and sunny, much like the day of her release and I was in the garden. My eyes were turned to every bird that flew. Then my heart leapt as I caught sight of a single buzzard over the nearby hills, not gliding but beating its large broad wings as it scanned the rough ground in search of food. I was not near enough to detect the detail of its feathers but the extremely large white areas under the wings, which Buzz possessed, showed up clearly as the bird twisted and turned in the skies. Recently the buzzards seen over Deer Close had been in twos and foursomes, and for once this was an immature single bird. Encouraged by this sight I looked forward with hope to longer and closer views in the days to come, as Buzz sailed by on the wind patrolling her territory around the cottage.

Many people have asked how, after such a close relationship with a wild creature, I can let it drift out of my life into the unknown. Many months of careful work go into the release of each bird or mammal and inevitably as I care for any living thing and see progress day by day, as the treatment or nursing overcomes the injury, I grow fond of my patients. Although I never tame any of them, I feel moved, after such close relationships, when I let them drift out of my life.

But wild creatures belong to the wild and I am adamant that no fit animal should be kept in captivity, so having done my best to prepare them to live their own life, I send them off into the unknown, knowing that because of their proved ability to catch their own particular food, their chances of survival are good.

In many cases their release is not into the unknown, and my greatest reward is to see them months or years later flying high or running free long after they have ceased to know me.

As I write, in February 1979, my work with birds and mammals continues unabated. Not a month passes without some injured bird—barn owl, kestrel, tawny owl, buzzard, sparrow hawk, little owl, long-eared owl or short-eared owl—coming to me for care. Last season I successfully launched twenty-three barn owls, bred from injured parents or reared in barns from second generation young, into the wild. One pair, introduced into a barn, raised seven healthy youngsters.

At the moment I am watching a third generation barn owl from one of my barn pairs. After flying free he collided one night with a car roof-rack and sustained multiple fractures of both wings. He was identified by his ring, returned to me, treated by my vet, nursed back to health over several months, and is now flying freely and strongly in a barn where I hope he will breed with another of my birds this spring.

Even the tiny insect-eating tree creeper has been nursed successfully after having had its wing torn by a cat. I returned it, much to its delight, to its oak tree in the woods and watched it resume its spiralling progress up the tree trunk in search of food. Straight away it found insects in the bark, before flying off to the next tree.

In two of my recent cases, I have treated a sparrow hawk and a short-eared owl with stiff wing joints. These developed after a fracture and damage to the nerves, so I have experimented with applied heat, massage and physiotherapy to bring back free movement and flight to birds that would otherwise never have flown again.

I have still not yet had success with the breeding of little owls and tawny owls. The eggs already laid have been infertile, but I have high hopes that this spring my injured pairs will prove compatible.

Many birds, particularly barn owls, will perish in this severe winter and my breeding programme will be more valuable than ever to help the numbers to recover.

More than sixty injured birds and a few mammals have passed through my hands in the last twelve months, and almost all have returned to full flight and freedom. As long as injured birds and mammals are there to be helped, I will continue my work.

Bibliography

Brock, D. W. E., *Foxhunting*, British Field Sports Society, 1973.
Burrows, R., *Wild Fox*, David & Charles Ltd., 1968.
Houston, J. M., *Country Topics*, Westmorland Gazette, 1976.
Lack, D., *Swifts in a Tower*, Chapman & Hall Ltd., 1956.
Pitt, F., *Hounds, Horses and Hunting*, Country Life, 1948.
Ratcliffe, E. J., *Through the Badger Gate*, G. Bell and Sons Ltd., 1974.
Ratcliffe, E. J., *A Badger returns to the Wild*, Animals, Vol. 13, no. 10, 1971.
Ratcliffe, E. J., *Seven Tawny Owls*, Animals 20, no. 3, 1973.
Ratcliffe, E. J., *Traffic Casualties, Barn Owls on the Decline*, Wildlife, Vol. 19, no. 8, 1977.
Ratcliffe, E. J., *Injured and Orphaned Birds of Prey Reared and Returned to the Wild*, Hawk Trust Report, 1974.
Ratcliffe, E. J., *Barn Owl Breeding for Return to the Wild*, Hawk Trust Report, 1975.
Ratcliffe, E. J., *Wildlife Consideration for the Highway Designer*, Chartered Municipal Engineer, Vol. 101, no. 11, 1974.
Ratcliffe, E. J., *Motorways and Badgers*, New Civil Engineer, Feb. 1973.
Sparks, J. and Soper, T., *Owls*, David & Charles Ltd., 1970.
Sharrock, J. T. R., *Atlas of Breeding Birds in Britain and Ireland*, British Trust for Ornithology, 1976.
Webster, J. A., *Seasonal Variation in Mammal Contents of Barn Owl Castings*, Bird Study, Vol. 20, no. 3, 1973, British Trust for Ornithology.
Vesey-Fitzgerald, B., *Town Fox, Country Fox*, André Deutsch Ltd., 1965.

Index